Skill Sharpeners 2

SECOND EDITION

Judy DeFilippo
Charles Skidmore

ADDISON-WESLEY PUBLISHING COMPANY

Reading, Massachusetts • Menlo Park, California
New York • Don Mills, Ontario • Wokingham, England
Amsterdam • Bonn • Sydney • Singapore • Tokyo • Madrid • San Juan

Judy DeFilippo is a coordinator of ESL in the Intensive English program at Northeastern University. She is author of *Lifeskills 1* and *2* and *Lifeskills and Citizenship,* and is co-author of *Grammar Plus,* all published by Addison-Wesley.

Charles Skidmore is an ESL teacher at the secondary level in the Boston, Massachusetts, schools and at Boston University's CELOP program. He is co-author of *In Good Company* also published by Addison-Wesley.

A Publication of the World Language Division

Editorial: Talbot Hamlin, Elly Schottman

Production/Manufacturing: James W. Gibbons

Illustrations: Elizabeth Hazelton, Kathleen Todd, publisher's files

Cover design: Marshall Henrichs, Richard Hannus

ISBN 0-201-51326-9
4 5 6 7 8 9 10 11 12 13-DA-96 95 94 93 92

Introduction

The *Skill Sharpeners* series has been especially designed for students whose skills in standard English, especially those skills concerned with reading and writing, require strengthening. It is directed both toward students whose first language is not English and toward those who need additional practice in standard English grammar and vocabulary. By introducing basic skills tied to classroom subjects in a simple, easy-to-understand grammatical framework, the series helps to prepare these students for success in regular ("mainstream") academic subjects. By developing and reinforcing school and life survival skills, it helps build student confidence and self esteem.

This second edition of *Skill Sharpeners* not only updates the content of many pages, it also provides increased focus for some of the grammar exercises and adds new emphasis on higher order thinking skills. In addition, there are more content-area readings, more biographies, new opportunities for students to write, and more practice in using formats similar to those of many standardized tests. The central purpose of the series remains the same, however. *Skill Sharpeners* remains dedicated to helping your students sharpen their skills in all facets of English communication.

With English as a Second Language students, *Skill Sharpeners* supplements and complements any basic ESL text or series. With these students and with others, *Skill Sharpeners* can also be used to reteach and reinforce specific skills with which students are having—or have had—difficulty. In addition, it can be used to review and practice grammatical structures and to reinforce, expand, and enrich students' vocabularies.

The grammatical structures in the *Skill Sharpeners* series follow a systematic, small-step progression with many opportunities for practice, review, and reinforcement. Vocabulary and skill instruction is presented in the context of situations and concepts that have an immediate impact on students' daily lives. Themes and subject matter are directly related to curriculum areas. Reading and study skills are stressed in many pages, and writing skills are carefully developed, starting with single words and sentences and building gradually to paragraphs and stories in a structured, controlled composition sequence.

If you are using *Skill Sharpeners* with a basic text or series, you may find that the structural presentation in *Skill Sharpeners* deviates from that in your text. In such a case, you should not expect most of your students to be able actively to use the structures on some pages in speaking or writing. The students should, however, be able to read and respond to the content. Do not be concerned about structural errors during discussion of the material. It is important that students become *actively involved* and *communicating*, however imperfectly, from the very beginning.

Using the *Skill Sharpeners*

Because each page or pair of pages of the *Skill Sharpeners* books is independent and self contained, the series lends itself to great flexibility of use. Teachers may pick and choose pages that fit the needs of particular students, or they may use the pages in sequential order. Most pages are self-explanatory, and all are easy to use, either in class or as homework assignments. Annotations at the bottom of each page identify the skill or skills being developed and suggest ways to prepare for, introduce, and present the exercise(s) on the page. In most cases, oral practice of the material is suggested before the student is asked to complete the page in writing. Teacher demonstration and student involvement and participation help build a foundation for completing the page successfully and learning the skill.

The *Skill Sharpeners* are divided into thematic units. The first unit of each book is introductory. In *Skill Sharpeners 1*, this unit provides exercises to help students say and write their names and addresses and to familiarize them with basic classroom language, school deportment, the names of school areas and school personnel, and number names. In later books of the series, the first unit serves both to review some of the material taught in earlier books and to provide orientation to the series for students coming to it for the first time.

At the end of each of the *Skill Sharpeners* books is a review of vocabulary and an end-of-book test of grammatical and reading skills. The test, largely in multiple-choice format, not only assesses learning of the skills but also provides additional practice for other multiple-choice tests.

The complete Table of Contents in each book identifies the skills developed on each page. A Skills Index at the end of the book lists skills alphabetically by topic and indicates the pages on which they are developed.

Skill Sharpeners invite expansion! We encourage you to use them as a springboard and to add activities and exercises that build on those in the books to fill the needs of your own particular students. Used this way, the *Skill Sharpeners* can significantly help to build the confidence and skills that students need to be successful members of the community and successful achievers in subject-area classrooms.

Contents

UNIT 4   Busy Lives

UNIT 5   Making Plans and Solving Problems

UNIT 6   Yesterday and Long Ago

UNIT 7   Yesterday and Today

UNIT 8   People and Places

UNIT 9   Agree and Disagree

UNIT 10   Reading Maps, Following Directions

UNIT 11   Our Country and Climate

Completing Forms

A. Answer the questions. Use short answers. The first one is done for you.

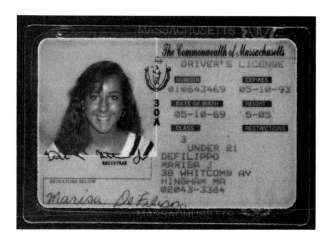

1. What is her first name?
   Marisa

2. What is her last name?
   _____

3. What is her address?
   _____

   _____

4. What is her license number?
   _____

5. What is her date of birth?
   _____

6. What is the expiration date?
   _____

B. Now complete the sentences about you, and fill in the form.

```
STUDENT I.D. CARD
              Please Print
Mr.   Miss
Mrs.  Ms.   Name _____
                    (last)      (first)      (middle)
Address: _____
                         (street)
_____
  (city)          (state)          (zip)
Home Telephone: _____  Sex: M  F

Native Country: _____ Date of Birth: _____

Signature: _____  Date: _____
```

1. My first name is
   _____

2. My address is _____
   _____

3. My date of birth is _____
   _____

4. My native country is _____
   _____

C. Write the dates.

1. 3–4–41   *March 4, 1941*
   mo. day year   _____

2. 10–10–66   _____

3. 8–30–79   _____

4. 1–21–09   _____

Skill Objectives: Reading a driver's license; completing identification forms; reading dates. *Part A:* Have the class read the driver's license. Teach or review vocabulary and abbreviations for address and dates (5-10-69). Have students answer the six questions. *Part B:* Have several students answer the four questions orally. Then go through the identification card line by line. Explain that I.D. is an abbreviation for identification. Show them how to circle the correct title (Mr., Miss, Mrs., Ms.) and be sure students understand what these stand for. *Part C:* Review this abbreviated way of writing dates. Point out that in the United States, the number for the month always comes first. Then assign for independent work.

Questions and Answers

Answer the following questions on a separate sheet of paper. Use complete sentences.

Set A

1. What is your first name?
2. What is your last name?
3. Do you have a nickname? What is it?
4. Where do you live?
5. How old are you?
6. What time do you wake up in the morning?
7. What time do you go to bed at night?
8. What time do you eat lunch on Monday?
9. What time do you eat lunch on Saturday?
10. What time do you eat dinner?
11. Where are you from?
12. What are you wearing today?
13. How many people are there in your family?
14. How many brothers do you have?
15. How many sisters do you have?
16. What is your favorite color?
17. What do you like to do after school?
18. What do you look like?
19. What is your telephone number?
20. What are some of your favorite foods?
21. What sports or games do you like to play?
22. What is your native language?

Set B

1. What letter comes before L in the alphabet?
2. What number comes after 7?
3. How many pennies are there in a dime?
4. How many dimes are there in a dollar?
5. How many nickels are there in a quarter?
6. What's the weather like today?
7. When do you use an umbrella?
8. What are the four seasons of the year?
9. What month comes after June?
10. What month comes before February?
11. How many states are there in the United States?
12. What are the four directions on a map?
13. What part of the country do you live in?
14. What day comes after Tuesday?
15. What day comes before Saturday?
16. Who takes care of sick people in a hospital?
17. What does a mechanic do?
18. How much does it cost to make a call in a phone booth?

10

Skill Objective: Reviewing basic grammar, vocabulary, and sentence structure. Students' answers to these questions will provide information about their language abilities at the present time. You may wish to do the page orally first, either as a class exercise or as pair work, and then assign it for written work in class or at home.

Match the Columns

Read carefully. Find the best word in Column B to go with Column A. Write it next to the word in Column A. The first one is done for you.

A		B
Country		**Language**
1. Australia	_English_	Greek
2. Mexico		Arabic
3. China		English
4. Greece		Portuguese
5. Brazil		Dutch
6. Saudi Arabia		Chinese
7. Netherlands		Spanish

Occupation		**Place**
1. teacher		restaurant
2. nurse		classroom
3. mail clerk		business office
4. secretary		orchestra
5. mechanic		hospital
6. chef		post office
7. musician		gas station

Food Item		**Food Category**
1. banana		meat
2. lemonade		dessert
3. corn		seafood
4. ice cream		poultry
5. roast beef		drink
6. clams		vegetable
7. fried chicken		fruit

Skill Objectives: Building vocabulary; classifying. Preview the vocabulary and teach or review any unfamiliar or difficult words. You may wish to do several items orally as a class before assigning the page for independent written work. Encourage students to use a dictionary if they encounter an unknown word. Discuss the completed page with the class. For additional practice, have students put the word pairs into question/answer form, for example, "In what country or countries do people speak English?" and ask and answer the questions with a partner.

The Wilson Family

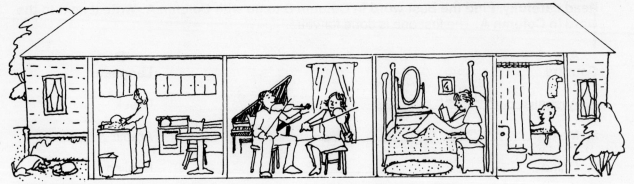

This is the Wilson family. Mr. and Mrs. Wilson are musicians. Right now, they are practicing the violin in the living room. Their son Bob isn't home now. He's taking piano lessons at the conservatory. Their daughter Lisa is in her bedroom. She's doing her home-work. Their daughter Gloria is in the kitchen now. She's washing the dishes. Their son Donald is in the bathroom. He's taking a bath. Their pets, Muffy the dog and Felix the cat, are in the yard. They are sleeping.

A. Read the story. Then read the sentences below. Write *T* if the sentence is true, write *F* is the sentence is false, and write *?* if the story doesn't give you the information. The first two are done for you as examples.

___F___ 1. Everyone in the Wilson family is at home today.

___?___ 2. Bob Wilson is a good piano player.

_____ 3. Mr. and Mrs. Wilson are practicing the violin.

_____ 4. Donald is washing the dishes.

_____ 5. Lisa's homework is easy.

_____ 6. Bob is at the conservatory.

_____ 7. Gloria likes to wash the dishes.

_____ 8. The pets are sleeping in the kitchen.

B. Write questions to go the answers.

1. _____ ? They are in the living room.

2. _____ ? They are practicing the violin.

3. _____ ? No, he isn't home.

4. _____ ? She's doing her homework.

5. _____ ? No, she isn't.

6. _____ ? He's taking a bath.

Skill Objectives: Reviewing present form of *to be*; present progressive; forming questions. Read the story aloud and have students locate each family member in the illustration; allow time for them to reread the story silently. *Part A:* Be sure students understand the directions clearly. Do the first two together and check that the class understands why the first item is marked *F* and why the second is marked with the question mark. *Part B:* Go through the items orally and be sure students are phrasing questions properly before you assign the page for independent written work.

What's for Lunch?

LUNCH MENU

pizza	hot dogs	hamburgers	tacos
fish	spaghetti	chop suey	chicken	lasagna
chocolate cake	apples	ice cream	grapes

---

1. Carla

   Carla likes tacos but she doesn't like pizza.

2. Rick

3. Tran and Nguyen

4. You

5.

6. Jim

7. Ana

8. Jan and Jill

Skill Objective: Present tense, third person singular: *likes/doesn't like.* Teach/review food vocabulary from the menu. Write and say: "I like pizza but I don't like hot dogs." Ask several students to state foods they like and dislike, then ask their classmates to recall these statements. Write the first answer on the board. "Carla likes tacos but she doesn't like pizza." Draw attention to the forms *likes* and *doesn't like.* Do the first three items on this page orally, as a class, then assign for independent work.

What Do You Like?

Use picture clues and diagrams to write sentences using like and like to.

A. Answer these questions. The first two are done for you as examples.

1. Do you like chicken? _Yes, I do. I like chicken._

2. Do you like fish? _No, I don't. I don't like fish._

3. Do you like pizza? _____

4. Do you like school? _____

5. Do you like rock music? _____

B. Study the grammar in the box. Then answer the questions.

| I, You, We, They | like to sing. | He, She, It | likes to sing. |

1. Do you like to watch TV? _Yes, I do. I like to watch T.V._

2. Do you like to do your homework? _____

3. Do you like to read? _____

4. Do you like to wash the dishes? _____

5. Do you like to go shopping? _____

C. Look at the pictures and answer the questions.

1. Does Lisa like to play soccer? _Yes, she does. She likes to play soccer._

2. Does Sue like to eat fish? _____

_____

 3. Does Paul like to dance? _____

_____

4. Do they like to clean the house? _____

_____

 5. Do they like to eat? _____

_____

Skill Objectives: Reviewing simple present tense; asking/answering questions with *Do/does . . . (like/like to).* Review the simple present tense, asking/answering questions with *Do/Does . . . (like, like to). Parts A, B, C:* Do all items orally before assigning as independent written work. Listen for correct use of *do/does* and *don't/doesn't.* As an extension, have each student write two questions beginning, "Do you like . . .?" Let a student begin the questioning, addressing any classmate he/she chooses. That classmate, after answering, may then direct one of his/her own questions to a third student.

Fannee Doolee's Secret

A. Fannee Doolee has a secret. She likes some things, but she doesn't like others. For example:

> She likes spoons, but she doesn't like forks.
> She likes eggs, but she doesn't like chickens.
> She likes chess, but she doesn't like checkers.

Do you know Fannee Doolee's secret? Tell which of these things she likes and which she doesn't like.

1. _She likes_ baseball.
2. _She doesn't like_ magazines.
3. _____ books.
4. _____ hockey.
5. _____ tennis.
6. _____ ping pong.
7. _____ lettuce.
8. _____ puppies.
9. _____ soccer.
10. _____ to fly.
11. _____ to dance.
12. _____ to cook.
13. _____ to dress up.
14. _____ to skate.
15. _____ to wake up early.
16. _____ to kiss.
17. _____ to read.
18. _____ to hurry.

B. Carlos Gonzales also likes some things and doesn't like others.

> He likes class, but he doesn't like school.
> He likes the Thames, but he doesn't like the Hudson.
> He likes Luis, but he doesn't like Jose.

Tell which things Carlos likes and which he doesn't like.

1. _He likes_ ducks.
2. _____ paper.
3. _____ gas.
4. _____ geese.
5. _____ meat.
6. _____ pets.

Now think of some of your own.

Carlos likes _____ but he doesn't like _____

_____

_____

_____

(*Clue:* Look at the spellings of the words. If you still aren't sure, look at page 124.)

Skill Objectives: Classifying; deductive thinking. Read the introductory lines aloud, then assign this puzzle page for independent work. Students who are stumped may refer to the clue written on the bottom of the page. Fannee's "secret" is at the bottom of page 124. As an extension activity, some students may enjoy creating their own secret classification and writing original "Things I Like" riddles.

A Conversation

A. Read the following conversation.

ROSA: Look at this white blouse, Janet.
JANET: Oh, it's pretty, Rosa. How much is it?
ROSA: It's on sale. Look at the price.
JANET: Twenty-two dollars. That's a very good price.
ROSA: Yes, it is. The regular price is forty-one dollars. I'm going to buy it.
JANET: Good. Let's pay for it and then go upstairs. I want to buy a blue dress for my cousin's party.

Answer the questions about the conversation. Circle the best answer. The first one is done for you.

1. Where are Janet and Rosa?
   a. in their house   b. at school   c. in a store

2. How much is the blouse Rosa wants?
   a. $22.00   b. $41.00   c. $24.00

3. How much money does Rosa save?
   a. $22.00   b. $19.00   c. $63.00

4. What color dress does Janet want?
   a. white   b. blue   c. red

5. Why is Janet looking for a new dress?
   a. She's buying it for her cousin.
   b. She wants to wear it to her cousin's party.
   c. Her cousin is Rosa.

B. Number the sentences below to show what people do when they shop for clothes in a store.

_____ They check the size and price.

_____ They pay for the clothing.

_____ They go into the store.

_____ They leave the store.

_____ They find something they like.

Skill Objectives: Reading for details; sequencing. *Part A:* Have students role-play the conversation or have them read it silently. Go over any new vocabulary. To be sure the students understand the multiple choice activity, do the first one together and discuss it. Be sure students understand that they should read all three possible answers before choosing one. *Part B:* Explain what students are to do. Have them read the sentences aloud and decide which sentence should be number 1. Then assign as independent work.

Reading a Graph

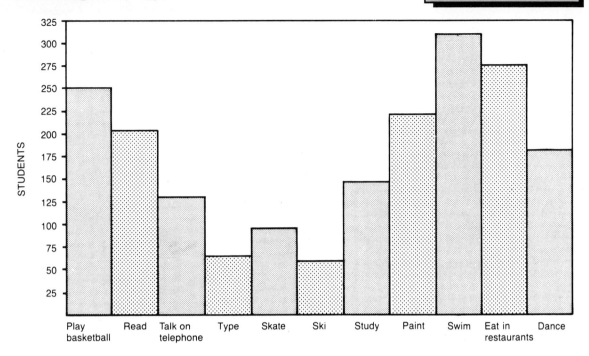

This graph gives the results of a survey of all 325 students at the Parker School to find out what activities they like.

A. Use the graph to decide if each of the following statements is True or False. Circle *T* if the statement is true. Circle *F* if it is false.

T F 1. Only fifty students like to type.

T F 2. All the students like to swim.

T F 3. Two hundred and fifty students like to play basketball.

T F 4. Skiing is very popular at the Parker School.

T F 5. More students like to paint than dance.

T F 6. More than one hundred students like to talk on the telephone.

T F 7. Two hundred and fifty students like to read.

T F 8. Fifty students do NOT like to eat in restaurants.

T F 9. More students like to dance than to read.

T F 10. More students like to swim than to skate.

T F 11. More than one hundred and fifty students do not like to study.

T F 12. Most students like to eat in restaurants.

T F 13. Only one hundred and fifty students like to dance.

T F 14. Fewer than one hundred students like to type.

T F 15. More than two hundred students like to swim.

B. Writing. On a separate sheet of paper, write about the students at the Parker School. Begin your composition with the following topic sentence:

The students at the Parker School like to do many different things.

Be sure to indent the first line of each paragraph, to begin each sentence with a capital letter, and to end each sentence with a period.

Skill Objective: Interpreting a bar graph. *Part A:* Read the directions aloud. Explain any unfamiliar words. Go over the data shown on the graph. For each entry, ask: "How many students like to . . .?" Using a ruler will help students read the graph. Encourage students to make comparative statements about the popularity of different activities: "More students like to . . . than to . . ." Assign Part A for independent work. Correct as a class. *Part B:* Review paragraph structure if necessary. Tell students that they can present the information in any order they wish. Assign for independent work.

What's Wrong?

Study the picture.

A. Can you find ten problems? Write them here. Find the words in the Data Bank. The first one is done for you.

1. *A man is eating a shoe.*

2. _____

3. _____

4. _____

5. _____

6. _____

7. _____

8. _____

9. _____

10. _____

D A T A B A N K

eating	drinking	wearing	playing	sleeping	reading	taking

B. Now, in paragraph form, describe what is happening in the restaurant. The topic sentence introduces the story. Use more paper if you need to.

Today is a crazy day at Ron's restaurant.

_____

_____

_____

_____

_____

_____

_____

Skill Objectives: Reviewing the present progressive; writing a paragraph from a picture. *Part A:* Have students discuss the picture and complete the ten items individually or in pairs. You may want to discuss why the items they have written are "problems" or "wrong." *Part B:* Explain topic sentence, concluding sentence, format. Then have students use the ten sentences from Part A to form a paragraph. Call attention to the fact that the first line is indented; remind students to use proper punctuation and capitalization.

Helping You Study:
The Table of Contents

The Table of Contents in a book is an important help to you in studying. The Table of Contents is a list of the chapters or units in the book. It tells you the name of the chapter and the page number for the first page of the chapter. Here is a sample Table of Contents from a beginner's book in English as a Second Language. Look at the Table of Contents and then answer the questions about it.

TABLE OF CONTENTS

Answer the questions. Use the Table of Contents to help you. The first one is done for you.

1. What chapter tells about meat, fruit, and vegetables? ____4____

2. What chapter tells about hats, coats, and dresses? _____

3. What chapter tells about brothers, sisters, and cousins? _____

4. What chapter tells about January, February, and March? _____

5. What chapter tells about feet, hands, and legs? _____

6. What chapter tells about rain, wind, and sun? _____

7. What chapter tells about the kitchen, living room, and dining room? _____

8. What chapter tells about school, the library, and the museum? _____

9. What chapter tells about football, baseball, and checkers? _____

10. What page is the first page of Chapter 5? _____

11. What page is the first page of Chapter 7? _____

12. What page is the first page of Chapter 11? _____

13. What page is the *last* page of Chapter 8? _____

14. What page is the last page of Chapter 3? _____

Skill Objectives: Using a table of contents; interpreting chapter titles. Go over the introductory paragraph and sample table of contents with the class. Answer some or all of the questions with the class before assigning the page as independent written work. As an extension activity, have students locate, examine, and ask each other questions about the tables of contents in several textbooks they are using.

Dear Dot

Dear Dot—

I have three older brothers, Ricky, Paul, and Sammy. I wear Ricky's old clothes. I use Paul's old bike, and I have Sammy's teacher in school this year. I want some new things, some things that belong only to me. I'm tired of hand-me-downs. What can I do?

Second-Hand Roberto

1. How many brothers does Roberto have? _____

2. Whose clothes does Roberto wear? _____

3. Whose bike does he use? _____

4. Whose teacher does he have? _____

5. What does Roberto want? _____

_____

6. What does the phrase *hand-me-downs* in this letter mean? Circle the best answer.

   a. new things   b. broken things   c. used things   d. hungry people

7. What is your advice to Roberto? Write a short answer. _____

_____

8. Now read Dot's answer. See if your answer is the same. If your answer is different, tell why you disagree. Dot's advice is below.

Dear Roberto—

There isn't very much you can do until you are older and you can earn enough money to buy your own things. For now, you can paint Paul's bike and put patches or labels on Ricky's old clothes. In school, do your best work for Sammy's old teacher. If you are her best student, she is sure to remember you and not Sammy.

Good luck,
Dot

What Do They Do?

Use what you already know to name and describe occupations.

A. Look at the pictures. Write the name of the occupation. Then write what the people do. The first one is done for you.

1. _He is a mail carrier._   _He delivers mail._

2. _____ _____

3. _____ _____

4. _____ _____

5. _____ _____

6. _____ _____

B. Circle the best answer.

1. A secretary _____ .
   a. teaches
   b. types
   c. sews

2. A teller _____ .
   a. cashes checks
   b. delivers mail
   c. drives a taxi

3. A pilot _____ .
   a. takes pictures
   b. works in a bank
   c. flies planes

4. A waitress _____ .
   a. cooks food
   b. serves food
   c. drives a bus

5. A hairdresser _____ .
   a. fixes cars
   b. cuts hair
   c. sells shoes

6. A construction worker _____ .
   a. cleans buildings
   b. builds buildings
   c. designs buildings

7. An astronaut _____ .
   a. travels in space
   b. fixes planes
   c. directs traffic

8. An electrician _____ .
   a. installs wiring
   b. fixes sinks
   c. cleans teeth

Skill Objectives: Reviewing the simple present tense; building vocabulary. *Part A:* Discuss the pictures and go through the six items orally. Be sure students pronounce the *s* in the third person singular. Then assign for independent written work. *Part B:* Review vocabulary as necessary. Do the first three or four items as a group, then assign as independent work.

21

What Do You Want to Be?

A. Write a sentence that tells what each one wants to be. The first one is done for you.

1.

   She wants to be a model.

2.

3.

4.

5.

6.

7.

8.

D A T A   B A N K

| actor | astronaut | carpenter | dancer | lawyer | model | singer |

B. Write a sentence that tells what each one wants to *do*. The first one is done for you.

1.

   He wants to play tennis.

2.

3.

Skill Objective: Present tense: *want(s) to.* Teach/review the occupation titles in the Data Bank. Then help students list as many other occupations as they can. Ask various students, "What do you want to be?" *Part A:* Have students offer sentences orally. Listen for correct use of *want/wants.* Assign for written work. *Part B:* Ask several students, "What do you want to do after school today?" Then ask classmates to recall these statements. "What does Carlos want to do?" Again, listen for correct use of *want/wants.* Assign for independent work.

Choosing a Career

I'm George. I like to help sick animals. I want to be a veterinarian. I have to take the college preparatory course in high school, and I have to attend college for four years. After that I have to attend a college of veterinary medicine for four more years!

Claudia and Armando like to play video games, and they like to use the computers in their high school. They want to design computers. In high school, they have to take the college course. Then they have to attend college. Many colleges now offer computer science programs.

Binh and Dao like to fix old radios and old cars. They want to be mechanics. They have to take a general course in high school or go to a vocational-technical school. They don't have to go to college.

Hiro also like computers. He wants to be a computer programmer. He is taking computer programming in high school. He doesn't have to go to college.

We like to help people. We want to be police officers. We have to be high school graduates, and we have to study for a civil service exam. When we pass the exam, we can apply for the job. Town or city officials appoint police officers. We can go to college for two years if we want to get an associate's degree in law enforcement.

My name is Lisa. I like to type and do secretarial work, but I want to work in a doctor's office. I want to be a medical secretary. I have to go to secretarial school for two years after high school, so it's a good idea to take the college preparatory course in high school. In secretarial school I plan to learn medical terminology. I also plan to learn how to use a word processor.

A. How about you? Write about what you want to be. Tell about the education you will need.

_____

_____

_____

_____

B. Now look at the following sentences. If a sentence is true, circle T. If it is false (not true), circle F.

1. You have to go to college to become a mechanic.   T   F

2. You have to go to junior college to become a computer programmer.   T   F

3. You have to take a civil service exam to become a police officer.   T   F

4. You have to attend college for eight years to become a veterinarian.   T   F

5. A computer designer needs only a high school education.   T   F

6. A mechanic can get training in a vocational-technical school.   T   F

7. You have to attend college for four years to become a medical secretary.   T   F

Skill Objectives: Using *like(s) to, want(s) to, have to*; reading for details; writing a paragraph. Read the paragraphs aloud. Explain any unfamiliar vocabulary. Allow time for students to reread silently. Have several students tell what they like to do and what they want to be. Let the class discuss the education needed. Let students complete this page independently. Correct the True/False questions together, then have volunteers read their paragraphs to the class.

What's Their Job?

A. Use the words in Data Bank A to complete each statement.

1. I can repair engines, install mufflers, change tires, and fix brakes.

   I am a _____

2. I take pictures and later develop those pictures. Newspapers use my pictures.

   I am a _____

3. I work in a department store. I help people find what they want. I use the cash register and give people receipts.

   I am a _____

4. I help people make wills. I write contracts. I help people who have to go to court. I help people get money that others owe to them.

   I am a _____

5. I can use an adding machine and a computer. I work with payrolls and send out paychecks.

   I am a _____

6. I help sick animals. People come to my office with their animals for regular checkups.

   I am a _____

DATA BANK A

bookkeeper   lawyer   veterinarian   mechanic   photographer   sales clerk

B. Here are some short paragraphs about different people. Put a title on each paragraph. Use Data Bank B for your titles. The first one is done for you.

1. *The Doctor*
He works in a hospital. He operates on sick people. He helps his patients. He knows a lot about medicine.

3. _____
She works in a hotel. She cleans up. She washes and polishes. She makes beds. She has a hard job.

2. _____
She works at a radio station. She plays records. She announces the news. She entertains people who listen.

4. _____
He works in a supermarket. He rings up the prices of food at his register. He packs the bags. He helps his customers.

DATA BANK B

The Disc Jockey   The Maid   The Doctor   The Cashier

C. Write a paragraph like the ones above about The Teacher.

_____

_____

_____

_____

Skill Objectives: Identifying topics; building vocabulary; drawing conclusions; writing a paragraph. *Part A:* Have students look at Data Bank A first to see how many occupations they already know. Have them explain them in their own words. Help with pronunciation if necessary. Have students do the first item as a group to be sure they understand the directions. Then assign as independent work. *Part B:* Follow the same procedure. *Part C:* Have students write a paragraph, similar to those in Part 2, about "the teacher." Before they write, discuss the various responsibilities of a teacher, writing them on the board as they are mentioned.

What, Where, and Why?

> The present progressive tense uses the verb *to be* and an *-ing* word.
>
> Examples: I am talking.   You are calling.   He is asking.
>   We are eating.   They are driving.

A. Use the present progressive form to help you answer each of the questions. The first one is done for you.

1. What is the mail carrier doing?

   He _____*is delivering*_____ the mail. (deliver)

2. What are the astronauts doing now?

   They _____ in space. (travel)

3. Is the pilot talking to the passengers?

   No, he _____ the plane. (fly)

4. What is the bank teller doing?

   She _____ a check. (cash)

5. Where's the waiter?

   He _____ food in the dining room. (serve)

6. Why are the photographers outside?

   They _____ pictures of a car accident. (take)

7. Are the sales clerks busy?

   No, they _____ in the aisles talking. (stand)

B. Use the present progressive to complete the following sentences. The first one is done for you.

1. The actors _____*are learning*_____ their lines. (learn)

2. The lawyer _____ to the judge. (talk)

3. The carpenters _____ a table. (make)

4. The police officer _____ the traffic. (stop)

5. You _____ a good job at the store. (do)

6. Ted _____ classes in computer programming. (take)

7. The singer _____ her new song. (practice)

Skill Objective: Reviewing the present progressive. Discuss the present progressive tense. Read the explanatory box to the students and review the present tense of *to be*. *Part A:* Do the first two items orally with the students; be sure students use the correct form of *to be*. *Part B:* Again check to be sure that students use the correct form of *to be*—that they equate "The actors" with "They" and "The lawyer" with "He" or "She." Then assign for independent work.

Present or Present Progressive?

Choose the correct tense to use in sentences.

> The present tense shows actions that happen repeatedly or EVERY day.
>
> The present progressive tense shows actions that are happening NOW.

Look at the following examples.

Present	Present Progressive
A mail carrier delivers the mail every day.	The mail carrier is delivering the mail now.
A teller cashes checks at a bank.	The teller is cashing my check now.
An electrician installs wiring.	The electrician is installing the wiring now.

Complete each sentence with the correct tense.

1. The astronauts _____ in space now.
   (are traveling, travel)

2. The pilot _____ to Brazil every Monday.
   (is flying, flies)

3. The waitresses _____ breakfast at the restaurant every morning.
   (are serving, serve)

4. The hairdresser _____ hair every day.
   (is cutting, cuts)

5. The secretary _____ the letter now.
   (is typing, types)

6. The carpenters _____ our house now.
   (are building, build)

7. A veterinarian _____ animals.
   (is taking care of, takes care of)

8. The police officer _____ the man now.
   (is arresting, arrests)

9. The sales clerks _____ a lot of fans every summer.
   (are selling, sell)

10. Doctors _____ their patients.
    (are helping, help)

11. The hairdresser is busy now; she _____ a customer's hair.
    (is cutting, cuts)

12. Disc jockeys _____ records on the radio.
    (are playing, play)

Skill Objective: Contrasting the present tenses. Discuss the grammar box and the examples; ask students for additional examples. The distinction between the tenses is difficult for many students to make. Do the entire page orally if students need the practice in either the grammer or pronunciation; then assign as independent written work.

26

Helping You Study:
Alphabetical Order (1)

A useful way of listing words is in alphabetical order. This means the order in which the words' first letters appear in the alphabet. For example, here is a list of words in alphabetical order:

apple   dinner   fly   jump   marry

Apple is first because its first letter, *a*, is the first letter in the alphabet. Dinner is next because its first letter, *d*, comes in the alphabet before the first letters of the other words. And so on.

A. Here are four lists of words that you know. Rewrite each list in alphabetical order. The first two words are done for you.

pig	*antelope*	teacher	_____
sheep	*cat*	plumber	_____
cat	_____	jeweler	_____
dog	_____	carpenter	_____
antelope	_____	farmer	_____

rice	_____	tennis	_____
tomato	_____	soccer	_____
chicken	_____	baseball	_____
fish	_____	hockey	_____
beans	_____	football	_____

B. When the words begin with the same letter, use the second letter to alphabetize. Rewrite each list in alphabetical order. The first two words have been done for you.

sweater	*shirt*	carrots	_____
shirt	*sleeve*	cheese	_____
socks	_____	celery	_____
sneakers	_____	cupcake	_____
sleeve	_____	cream	_____

DATA BANK

A B C D E F G H I J K L M N O P Q R S T U V W X Y Z

Helping You Study:
Alphabetical Order (2)

A. When words start with the same two letters, you have to use the third letter to put them in alphabetical order. **Write each of these lists in alphabetical order.**

cheese _____   spoon _____

chocolate _____   spring _____

change _____   speak _____

church _____   splash _____

chicken _____   spy _____

B. **Now try these long columns. Be careful. Sometimes you are going to have to use second, third, or even fourth letters.**

Column A		Column B	
dog	_____	museum	_____
purple	_____	read	_____
floor	_____	not	_____
square	_____	sister	_____
black	_____	last	_____
make	_____	parts	_____
armchair	_____	snow	_____
man	_____	now	_____
swim	_____	quarter	_____
gloves	_____	throat	_____
pilot	_____	late	_____
uncle	_____	rug	_____
blast	_____	parents	_____
warm	_____	thumb	_____
blond	_____	lawyer	_____
jacket	_____	pants	_____

Skill Objective: Alphabetizing. Read the directions to Part A aloud. If you wish, have a volunteer write the alphabet on the board for student reference. Alphabetize the first column of words as a class. Assign the rest of the page for independent work. For additional practice in this skill, write the names of the months on the board and have students alphabetize these twelve words.

Dear Dot

Dear Dot—

My boyfriend, Dennis, likes cars. He reads about cars, talks about cars, thinks about cars, and probably dreams about them too. He wants to be a mechanic when he finishes school. All of that is okay with me, but there is one problem. Dennis drives too fast. He thinks that he knows everything about cars, and that nothing can happen to us. I know we are going to have an accident soon. Sometimes he drives over eighty miles an hour. What can I do?

Nervous

1. What does Dennis like? _____

2. What does Dennis want to be? _____

3. What is Nervous's problem? _____

_____

4. Why does Dennis drive fast? _____

_____

5. What does the word *accident* in this letter mean? Circle the best answer.

   a. mistake   b. crash   c. murder   d. problem

6. What is your advice to Nervous? Write a short answer._____

_____

7. Now read Dot's answer. See if your answer is the same. If your answer is different, tell why you disagree. Dot's advice is below.

Dear Nervous—

You can stay out of Dennis's car. More than 8,000 teenagers die every year in car accidents in the United States. They die because too many teenagers drive too fast, and drive after drinking alcohol. You have to protect yourself. Tell your boyfriend you are not going to ride with him until he slows down. And when you do start to ride with him, remember to wear your seat belt!

Dot

Skill Objectives: Reading comprehension; understanding words through context; making judgments. Read the letter aloud to the class, then have them reread it silently. Have students answer questions 1-6. Correct the first five questions as a class. Encourage discussion of question 6, then have students write their answers to it. Have them read Dot's answer and discuss how it agrees and disagrees with their own advice to Nervous.

What Do You Do, Henriette?

There are some things that Henriette always does. There are other things she never does. And there are things that she does sometimes but doesn't do other times. This chart shows how frequently Henriette does certain things.

How Often

	Always	Often	Sometimes	Seldom	Never
1. telephone her mother			✔		
2. go to the movies				✔	
3. play tennis on weekends		✔			
4. read the newspaper	✔				
5. eat out			✔		
6. go to the opera					✔
7. give a party				✔	
8. clean the apartment on Saturday	✔				
9. listen to rock music					✔
10. take a vacation in Miami			✔		
11. travel to New York		✔			
12. go fishing					✔

Write sentences that tell how often Henriette does each thing in the list. Use the chart. The first sentence is done for you.

1. *Henriette sometimes telephones her mother.*

2. _____

3. _____

4. _____

5. _____

6. _____

7. _____

8. _____

9. _____

10. _____

11. _____

12. _____

Skill Objectives: Interpreting a chart; understanding adverbs of frequency; third person singular present tense. Read the introductory paragraph aloud. Study the chart with the class. Have students name things Henriette does always, often, etc. Do the written exercise orally, as a group, before assigning as independent work. As an extension, help the class create a similar activity chart. Each student can fill out the chart with information about him/herself. Students can then exchange charts and write sentences about each other.

30

Odd Man Out

A. Odd Man Out. Circle the word that doesn't belong. The first one is done for you.

1. bus, train, (house,) plane
2. potato, lamb, pork, beef
3. soccer, basketball, football, checkers
4. drum, window, piano, flute
5. comic book, newspaper, ball, magazine
6. fish, coffee, milk, lemonade
7. sweater, pants, gloves, door
8. pineapple, lettuce, orange, banana
9. sofa, table, kitchen, chair
10. roast beef, breakfast, lunch, dinner
11. November, December, July, Sunday
12. teeth, men, children, foot
13. eyes, hands, nose, mouth
14. cup, hammer, saw, pliers
15. Chinese, French, English, United States

B. Read each statement. Decide if it is about something that happens always, or often, or seldom, or never. Then write one of these words next to each statement: always, often, seldom, never. The first one is done for you.

1. Dogs speak English. _____*never*_____

2. The sun rises in the east. _____

3. People walk on the moon. _____

4. Money grows on trees. _____

5. Spaceships from Mars visit the earth. _____

6. Drunken drivers cause accidents on the roads._____

C. Write a sentence of your own for each one of these words.

(always) _____

(often) _____

(seldom) _____

(never) _____

Skill Objectives: Classifying; using adverbs of frequency. Do several examples in each part as a class, then let students complete the page independently. Correct and discuss the answers together. For Part A, let students explain why three of the words are alike, and why the fourth word does not belong. Correct Part B as a class. Let each student read his/her favorite sentence from Part C.

31

A Busy Place

There is always a lot of activity in the emergency room of a large hospital. People are always coming and going. Most of the people who come to an emergency room are accident victims. They usually have cuts, broken bones, or burns. They want help right away.

Unfortunately, these people often have to wait to see a doctor. They have to fill out information forms about hospital insurance and medical history. After they complete these forms, they can see one of the doctors. Of course, if there is a crowd, everyone has to wait for his or her turn.

Sometimes people come to the hospital by ambulance. These are often life-or-death situations. These patients seldom have to fill out forms or wait for their turn. They need quick medical attention. The doctors almost always see them right away.

Doctors, nurses, technicians, and secretaries try to work as fast as possible in the emergency room. They know that there is always something to do or someone to take care of. Working in an emergency room is a difficult and tiring job. There is never a dull or quiet moment.

A. Read the story. Then answer the questions. Use complete sentences. The first one is done for you.

1. Who are most of the people who come to an emergency room? _____

    _____ *They are accident victims.* _____

2. What problems do they have? _____

    _____

3. What do people in an emergency room want? _____

    _____

4. What do most of the people have to do before they see a doctor? _____

    _____

5. How do some people come to the hospital? _____

    _____

6. Why do the people in the emergency room work fast? _____

    _____

7. Why is it difficult to work in an emergency room? _____

    _____

B. What is the story mostly about? Circle the best answer.

   a. sick people   b. doctors and nurses   c. ambulances   d. emergency rooms

Skill Objectives: Identifying main idea and details; understanding adverbs of frequency. Read the story aloud. Explain any unfamiliar vocabulary. Let students discuss experiences they have had with emergency rooms. Ask students to reread the story silently. You may wish to cover a few questions as a group before assigning the page as independent work. Correct and discuss the answers together. Encourage volunteers to explain why "emergency rooms" is the correct answer to Part B.

32

Cashing a Check

Julio Ayala is 14. After school and on weekends, Julio babysits for three different families. Julio is a good babysitter, and the children love him. Sometimes Julio receives cash. And sometimes he receives a check.

Do you have a job after school or on weekends? Do you receive checks?

A. Here is one of Julio's checks. Look at it and then answer the questions about it.

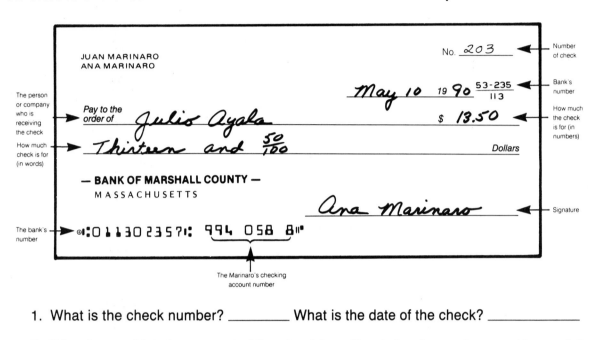

1. What is the check number? _____ What is the date of the check? _____

2. Why do you think the amount of the check is written twice, in numbers and in words?

   _____

3. Why do you think there are two names in the upper left corner of the check?

   _____

4. How much is the check for? _____

5. What is the Marinaros' account number? _____

B. To cash the check, Julio must endorse it, that is, sign his name on the back of it. Then he can get cash for the check. Julio always cashes his checks at a store where people know him. Other stores will not let him cash checks there.

   1. Why do you think Julio has to endorse the check to cash it? _____

   _____

   2. Why do you think stores that do not know Julio won't let him cash checks there?

   _____

   _____

Skill Objectives: Reading a check; understanding bank procedures. Read the introductory paragraphs aloud. Let the class discuss the questions posed at the end. How many students have received checks? What did they do with them? How many have checking accounts? *Part A:* Examine the check as a class. Let students answer the questions orally. *Part B:* Allow time for students to answer these questions independently. Then have the class compare answers and discuss the problems.

33

A Savings Account

Learn how to start a savings
account and read its passbook.

Julio Ayala puts part of his babysitting money into a savings account in a bank. The bank pays him interest for the use of his money. It adds the interest to his account each month.

To open a bank account like Julio's, you have to fill out a signature card. On this card you write your name, address, and social security number. Some banks also ask you to write your mother's name before she was married. This is to protect you. Another person who tries to take money out of your bank account is not likely to know this information.

You write your signature on the card. The bank checks this signature with the signature on each request to take money out of the account to make sure that the request is from you.

A. When you open a savings account, you receive a passbook. Every time you put money into the account or take money out of it, the teller lists this in the passbook. The teller also lists the interest that the account earns. **Here is part of a page from Julio's passbook. Use it to answer the questions.**

	DATE	WITHDRAWAL	DEPOSIT	INTEREST	BALANCE	TELLER
1	1/10/91		11.00	.25	63.25	0213
2	2/2/91		8.00	.30	71.55	0213
3	2/15/91		15.00		86.55	0212
4	3/3/91		7.00	.42	93.97	0211
5	3/21/91	25.00			68.97	0213
6	4/1/91		12.50	.38	81.85	0212

1. How much money is in the account on April 1, 1991? _____

2. How much is Julio's deposit of February 15? _____

3. How much did Julio withdraw on March 21? _____

4. How much is the interest for the period shown here? _____

B. Here is a signature card to open a savings account. Fill it out for yourself or for a made-up person.

Why do you think there are places for two names?

_____

_____

_____

_____

No.		The undersigned hereby agree to the By-laws of the BOXTOWN SAVINGS BANK relating to savings deposits now or hereafter in force and agree(s) to the regulations governing the use of this account and acknowledge(s) receipt of a copy of said regulations.

☐ SINGLE ACCOUNT ☐ JOINT ACCOUNT

#1 Sign here	#2 Sign here
Print name here	Print name here
Social Security number	Social Security number
Telephone number	Telephone number
Number Street Apt. #	Number Street Apt. #
City, State, Zip code	City, State, Zip code
Date of birth	Date of birth
Mother's maiden name	Mother's maiden name
For bank use only-ID	For bank use only-ID
DATE / OPENED BY	DATE / OPENED BY

Skill Objectives: Learning about savings accounts; understanding entries in a passbook. Read the introductory paragraphs aloud. Discuss unfamiliar vocabulary and concepts. *Part A:* Examine the passbook page together. Have students practice reading the dates and describing the activity that took place in the account that day. (The teller number identifies the person at the bank who helped Julio with the transaction.) *Part B:* Discuss what a joint account is and provide help as needed; students will fill out only the left part of the signature card. Correct and discuss answers with the class.

34

A Student Survey

This chart shows the results of a survey of one hundred students asking how often they do different things. The numbers on the chart show how many students do each thing never, sometimes, usually, often, or always.

Number of Students

	Never	Sometimes	Usually	Often	Always
1. Help your mother.	2	16	25	30	27
2. Wash the dishes.	22	20	20	15	23
3. Empty the trash.	12	30	15	18	25
4. Make your bed.	5	26	20	36	13
5. Do your homework.	2	19	30	30	19
6. Get up at 5:30.	89	10	1	0	0
7. Buy school lunch.	24	14	26	26	10
8. Read school newspapers.	3	30	20	20	27
9. Speak English at home.	12	20	5	5	58
10. Cook your own supper.	44	10	21	15	10

Use the chart to answer the questions. The first one is done for you.

1. How many students usually do their homework? _____ *30 usually do.*

2. How many students never wash the dishes? _____

3. How many students always make their beds? _____

4. How many students sometimes buy school lunches? _____

5. How many students usually get up at 5:30? _____

6. How many students often empty the trash? _____

7. How many students always speak English at home? _____

8. How many students never read school newspapers? _____

9. How many students usually cook their own supper? _____

10. How many students sometimes help their mother? _____

11. How many students always get up at 5:30? _____

12. How many students never do their homework? _____

13. How many students usually speak English at home? _____

14. How many students never empty the trash? _____

Skill Objectives: Interpreting a chart; using adverbs of frequency. Ask questions about the information on this chart, first having students refer to each statistic in order ("How many students never/sometimes/often . . . help their mother?"), then having them use the grid to locate scattered information. ("How many students usually buy lunch/never get up at 5:30/etc.?") Let students ask each other questions. Assign the page for independent work. Students can use this chart as a questionnaire form for their own class. They can then tabulate and report the results.

35

Is That A Fact?

Here are some statements about Thanksgiving. Decide whether each is a fact or an opinion. Remember that facts are true statements that you can read or check in an encyclopedia or other reference book. Opinions are what a person thinks about something. They are true for the person, but they may not be true for other people.

Read each statement. Write FACT if the statement is a fact. Write OPINION if it is an opinon.

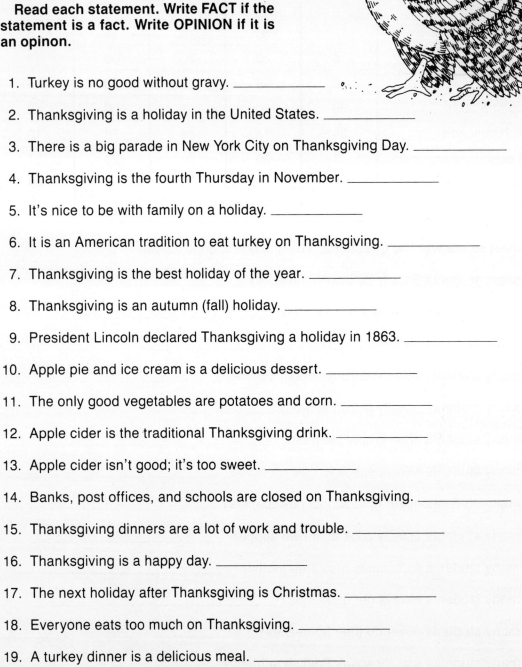

1. Turkey is no good without gravy. _____

2. Thanksgiving is a holiday in the United States. _____

3. There is a big parade in New York City on Thanksgiving Day. _____

4. Thanksgiving is the fourth Thursday in November. _____

5. It's nice to be with family on a holiday. _____

6. It is an American tradition to eat turkey on Thanksgiving. _____

7. Thanksgiving is the best holiday of the year. _____

8. Thanksgiving is an autumn (fall) holiday. _____

9. President Lincoln declared Thanksgiving a holiday in 1863. _____

10. Apple pie and ice cream is a delicious dessert. _____

11. The only good vegetables are potatoes and corn. _____

12. Apple cider is the traditional Thanksgiving drink. _____

13. Apple cider isn't good; it's too sweet. _____

14. Banks, post offices, and schools are closed on Thanksgiving. _____

15. Thanksgiving dinners are a lot of work and trouble. _____

16. Thanksgiving is a happy day. _____

17. The next holiday after Thanksgiving is Christmas. _____

18. Everyone eats too much on Thanksgiving. _____

19. A turkey dinner is a delicious meal. _____

20. The Pilgrims celebrated the first American Thanksgiving. _____

Skill Objective: Distinguishing between fact and opinion. Read and discuss the explanation on the top of the page. All the facts and opinions in this activity refer to Thanksgiving. Let the students briefly discuss what they know about this holiday. Complete and discuss several examples on this page as a class. Be sure students understand that none of the sentences are false. When students are secure with the concept, assign the page for independent work. Correct and discuss as a class.

Have or Has?

Use a diagram and a story to help you understand have and has.

| I You We They | > have | He She It | > has |

A. Fill in the blanks with *have* or *has*.

1. —How are you today?

   —Terrible. I _____ a headache.

2. —How is Lisa?

   —Terrible. She _____ an earache.

3. —How is Jim?

   —Terrible. He _____ a bad cold.

4. —How are they?

   —Terrible. They _____ the flu.

5. —How is your dog?

   —Terrible. It _____ a broken leg.

6. —How are you?

   —Terrible. I _____ a stomachache.

B. Read the following story about the Ruiz family. Then answer the questions by writing *Yes* or *No*.

This is the Ruiz family. Mr. and Mrs. Ruiz have three children, Lisa, Rosa, and Roberto, and two pets, a dog and a cat. In the summer, the children always have fun together at the beach. They seldom have trouble finding friends to go with them. Lisa never has enough time for all the things she wants to do. Mr. Ruiz usually has dinner waiting when they get home. In the evening, Rosa often has a date with one of her boyfriends, and Roberto sometimes has a chess game with his mother.

1. Do Mr. and Mrs. Ruiz have two children? _____

2. Do Mr. and Mrs. Ruiz have two pets? _____

3. Do the Ruiz children have a good time together? _____

4. Do they have trouble finding friends? _____

5. Does Lisa usually have enough time? _____

6. Does Rosa have more than one boyfriend? _____

7. Does Lisa usually have dinner waiting? _____

8. Does Mrs. Ruiz know how to play chess? _____

C. Complete the following sentences with *have* or *has*.

1. Richard _____ a new car.

2. Mary _____ brown eyes.

3. We _____ many friends in Miami.

4. My dog _____ a short tail.

5. The house _____ eight rooms.

6. Tom and Helen _____ red hair.

7. She and I _____ fun in school.

8. Cesar _____ a bad temper.

Skill Objectives: Present forms of *to have*; reading for details. Review the verb chart at the top of the page. Go over the directions for all three parts. You may wish to do one or more examples as a class, before assigning the page for independent work.

37

Helping You Study: Using the Dictionary (1)

The words in a dictionary are in alphabetical order. You know that words that begin with the letter *c*, for example, come after words that begin with the letter *b*, and that words that begin with *w* come after words that begin with *u* or *v*.

But you don't have to go through all the pages before the words that begin with *w* to look up the word *waver,* for example. You need only look in the right section of the dictionary.

Look in the **front** section of the dictionary for words that begin with **A,B,C,D,E,F,** and **G.**

Look in the **middle** section of the dictionary for words that begin with **H,I,J,K,L,M,N,O,** and **P.**

Look in the **back** section of the dictionary for words that begin with **Q,R,S,T,U,V,W,X,Y,** and **Z.**

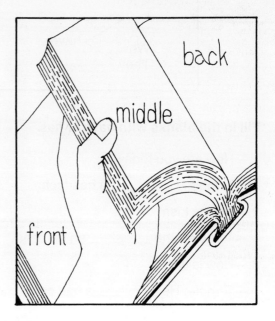

A. Tell what section of the dictionary these words are in. The first one is done for you.

1. tomorrow __back__	8. tooth _____	15. executive _____
2. please _____	9. architect _____	16. yellow _____
3. elbow _____	10. kitchen _____	17. jacket _____
4. bad _____	11. wet _____	18. concert _____
5. green _____	12. store _____	19. middle _____
6. office _____	13. beans _____	20. train _____
7. window _____	14. hair _____	21. island _____

B. Answer the questions. Write *before* or *after*.

1. Is "ape" before or after "zebra" in the dictionary? _____

2. Is "kitchen" before or after "cook" in the dictionary? _____

3. Is "milk" before or after "cow" in the dictionary? _____

4. Is "top" before or after "bottom" in the dictionary? _____

5. Is "chicken" before or after "egg" in the dictionary? _____

Skill Objective: Approximating the location of a word in the dictionary. Read the explanatory sentences at the top of the page aloud. Do a number of examples from Parts A and B as a group, then assign the page as independent work. Correct as a class. As an extention activity, provide students with dictionaries and organize a dictionary race. Hold up a word on a flashcard. The first student to find the word must read the definition aloud. Score can be kept by giving points to individuals or to teams.

38

Dear Dot

Dear Dot—

I am the only girl in my family. I have four brothers. I almost always do the dishes and wash the clothes. My mother works, so I often do the cooking, too. My brothers almost never help clean the house, and they always mess it up. I am tired of doing all the work in the house. What can I do?

Cinderella

1. How many children are in Cinderella's family? _____

2. What does she almost always do? _____

   _____

3. Why does she do the cooking? _____

4. What do her brothers almost never do? _____

   _____

5. What does the phrase *mess up* in this letter mean? Circle the best answer.

   a. make dirty   b. make clean   c. destroy   d. help

6. What is your advice for Cinderella? Write a short answer. _____

   _____

7. Now read Dot's answer. See if your answer is the same. If your answer is different, tell why you disagree. Dot's advice is below.

Dear Cinderella—

You need some help. You have to have a family meeting. Talk to your mother and your brothers. Tell them how much work you are doing and how little work your brothers are doing. Make a chart or write a list of things to do and give everyone a job. Ask your mother to check to see who is and who isn't doing their job. You don't have to do all the work in your house. Your brothers should help you.

Good luck,
Dot

Skill Objectives: Reading comprehension; understanding words through context; making judgments. Read the letter aloud as students follow along. Define any unfamiliar words. Explain the fairy tale character, Cinderella. Ask students if a similar story is told in their native country. Ask, "Why does this letter writer sign herself Cinderella?" Have students reread the letter silently, then answer the questions. Correct answers as a class. Have students compare and discuss their own advice and Dot's replay. Encourage lively discussion.

Dr. Rubin's Busy Schedule

6:30	gets up
6:40	takes a shower
6:50	gets dressed
7:00	has juice, toast, and coffee for breakfast
7:15	leaves her apartment
7:30	arrives at the hospital
7:45	visits patients in the hospital
9:15	arrives at her office, sees patients with appointments
12:00	has lunch
1:00	sees more patients with appointments
3:30	drives to the university (two days a week)
4:00	teaches class (two days a week)
6:00	arrives home

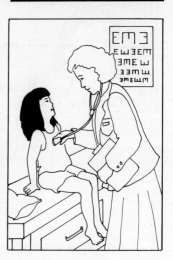

Read Dr. Rubin's daily schedule. Then write questions about her. The answer to each question is at the right. The question you write has to go with this answer. The first word or words of each question are at the left. The first question is done for you.

1. What time _does she get up_ ? She gets up at 6:30.

2. Does _____ ? Yes, she does.

3. What _____ ? She has juice, toast, and coffee.

4. When _____ ? She leaves at 7:15.

5. How long _____ ? It takes her 15 minutes to get to the hospital.

6. How long _____ ? She visits patients for 1 1/2 hours.

7. What _____ ? After visiting patients, she goes to her office.

8. Why _____ ? To see patients with appointments.

9. When _____ ? She eats lunch at 12:00.

10. Does _____ ? No, she sees only patients who have appointments.

11. When _____ ? She drives there at 3:30.

12. Does _____ ? No, she only goes there two days a week.

13. Why _____ ? To teach a class there.

14. Does _____ ? No, she arrives home at 6:00.

Skill Objectives: Third person singular, simple present tense; asking questions. Have students read and discuss the doctor's daily routine. Do the first five items with the class, asking for volunteers to phrase questions 2 through 5. Then assign the page for independent work. When students have completed the page, have students compare their questions.

40

Things People Do

I like	You ask	We dance	They push
He ⟍	The boy ⟍	My friend ⟍	This man ⟍
She —likes	The girl —asks	Your friend —dances	That woman —pushes
It ⟋	The question ⟋	The bear ⟋	A snowplow ⟋

To change most verbs to the third person singular, just add s. If the verb ends in s, x, ch, or sh, add es. The es ending stands for the sound "iz." When s follows the letters ce, ge, or se, it is also pronounced "iz."

A. Complete the sentence by writing the correct form of the underlined verb. The first one is done for you.

1. Those children <u>like</u> cats. This child ___*likes*___ dogs.

2. John and Mary <u>walk</u> to school together. Tomás _____ to school alone.

3. My brothers and I <u>watch</u> TV every night. Michelle _____ TV only on Thursdays.

4. My mother and father <u>drive</u> very carefully. My sister _____ too fast.

5. The eighth graders <u>want</u> to win the race. Nobody _____ to lose.

6. The Smoots <u>wash</u> their clothes on Sunday. Mrs. Perez _____ on Friday.

7. Good friends <u>call</u> each other often. My friend Molly _____ me every day.

8. I <u>change</u> my clothes when I get home from school. Erica _____ her clothes, too.

B. Read the paragraph below. Write the missing words on the line. Use the verbs in the Data Bank. Add s or es to each verb. The first one is done for you.

Ramon Medina ___*loves*___ to exercise. He is a physical fitness "nut." Every morning he

_____ forty laps in the school swimming pool. In the afternoon he _____ basketball

with his friends. Three times a week he _____ five miles. On Saturday mornings he

_____ weights and _____ rope. On Saturday afternoons he _____ on boxing

gloves and _____ with some of the guys at the gym. Sunday is Ramon's day for bicy-

cling. He _____ his bike for miles until he _____ a nice spot for a picnic. On Sun-

day nights, Ramon _____ home. He _____ sports on television!

D A T A   B A N K

box	find	jump	lift	love	play
put	ride	run	stay	swim	watch

Skill Objective: Constructing third person singular present tense: -s, -es. Read the example box aloud. Have students note how the spelling of each verb changes in the third person singular. Have them note the sound represented by each final s or es. Go over the rules together. Write on the board: *I use, I fix, I want, I brush, I bake.* Have volunteers change these to third person singular. Ask each student to use one of the verbs in a sentence. Do Part A orally before assigning the page as independent work.

41

How They Live: Two Stories

Use what you know to choose the right forms of the verbs in the sentences.

Read the two stories below. Complete the sentences with words from the Data Bank. Watch for singular and plural subjects. Add s or es to the verbs in the Data Bank when needed. The first word has been filled in for you.

The Martin Family

Rene and Henriette Martin _____*live*_____ in Miami. Rene _____ in a hospital. Henriette _____ a dress shop. She _____ a lot of time in the store. The Martins _____ two children, Guy and Therese. Both children _____ the Traymore Vocational School. Guy _____ to be a plumber when he _____ school. Therese _____ on becoming an electrician. Mr. and Mrs. Martin _____ sure that their children _____ hard in school. They want their daughter and son to be successful.

DATA BANK

attend	finish	have	hope	live	make	own	plan	spend	study	work

David Colon

David Colon is a professional photographer. He _____ all around the world. He _____ pictures of politicians and movie stars. David _____ the celebrities to look natural. He _____ his camera quickly. He _____ his subjects yawning and laughing, looking thoughtful or surprised. Most famous people _____ publicity; they _____ having their pictures taken. However, some celebrities _____ to avoid David's camera. They _____ to stay out of the public eye as much as possible. David _____ his pictures to newspapers and magazines. Newspapers and magazines _____ lots of money for photographs of famous people, especially the ones who are "camera shy."

DATA BANK

catch	enjoy	like	pay	prefer	sell	take	travel	try	use	want

Skill Objectives: Constructing the present tense; choosing the correct form. Review the rules presented on page 41. If appropriate, provide additional oral practice with the skill. Read and complete the first few sentences of "The Martin Family" as a class, then assign the page for independent work. Correct the page orally, asking volunteers to read the completed sentences aloud.

Writing About Work

Margo and Allison are nurses at Central Hospital. They work in the pediatric, or children's, ward. They enjoy their work, and they take excellent care of the children. They carry trays with food and medicine. They check temperatures and give shots. They watch each child's condition carefully, and notify the doctor of his or her progress. Margo and Allison are kind and patient. They smile and try to make the children feel comfortable. They know that a hospital can be a frightening place for a child.

A. What is the main idea of this story? Circle your answer.

a. Margo and Allison enjoy their work with the children.

b. Margo and Allison do many things to help children in the hospital.

c. Margo and Allison are kind and patient with the children.

d. A hospital can be a frightening place for children.

B. Now write the same story about Linda, who is also a nurse. She works with Margo and Allison in the pediatric ward. Use the following rule:

I cry   He
         She ⟩ cries
         It

I play   He
         She ⟩ plays
         It

When the first person singular form of a verb ends in a consonant followed by *y*, change the *y* to *ies* to make the third person singular. When the first person singular form of the verb ends in a vowel followed by *y*, just add *s* to make the third person singular. In both cases you pronounce (say) the word just as you pronounce the first person form but with a *z* sound at the end of it.

Write your story about Linda below. The first sentence is done for you.

Linda is a nurse at Central Hospital.

_____

_____

_____

_____

_____

_____

_____

Skill Objectives: Third person singular present tense: *-s, -es, -ies*; identifying main idea. Read the paragraph aloud. Explain new words. Allow students to reread silently, then answer Part A. Discuss why choice *b* is the best answer. *Part B:* Review the verb rule with the students. Write on the board: *pay, stay, hurry, annoy, fly.* Ask volunteers to write the third person singular of each verb. Ask others to use the verbs in oral sentences. You may wish to do the exercise as an oral activity before assigning as written work.

43

Whose Is It?

A. **Use the chart above to answer these questions. Answer in complete sentences.** The first ones are done for you.

1. Whose umbrella is it? _It's Amy's umbrella._

2. Whose golf clubs are they? _They're Amy's golf clubs._

3. Whose cat is it? _____

4. Whose shoes are they? _____

5. Whose pen is it? _____

6. Whose books are they? _____

7. Whose car is it? _____

8. Whose records are they? _____

B. **Read each sentence. Then write the right word in the blank:** *his, my, our, her* or *their.*

1. She washes _____her_____ hair every day.

2. Fred wants to borrow _____ father's car.

3. Bob and I cook _____ dinner together.

4. Do you want to do _____ homework now?

5. My sister is looking for _____ keys.

6. The Browns are painting _____ house.

7. I seldom drive _____ car.

8. John and Bill are doing _____ laundry at the laundromat.

9. Linda and I are watching _____ favorite TV program.

The Post Office

Ann Jenkins is a mail carrier. She carries mail in her bag and delivers letters. Some mail carriers walk. Some drive small trucks or jeeps.

Henry Gavin is a postal clerk. He works in the post office. He sells stamps, insures packages, and issues money orders. A money order is similar to a check.

Not all towns have mail carriers. In some small towns, people have a box at the post office. They have to pick up their mail every day.

Post Offices provide other important services. Americans can get passports through the post office. Aliens (citizens of other countries) report their American addresses on January first to the post office. The post office gives that information to the Immigration and Naturalization Service.

If you send a letter to somebody nearby or in the same state, that letter usually travels by truck. If you send a letter a longer distance, from Florida to California, for example, that letter travels by plane, but you don't need an airmail stamp. Airmail stamps are necessary only when you send a letter outside of the United States.

Read the story. Then look at the sentences below. Write a _T_ if the sentence is true. Write an _F_ if the sentence is false. Write a _?_ if the story doesn't give you enough information to tell whether the sentence is true or false. The first two are done for you.

_T_ 1. Aliens are citizens of another country.

_?_ 2. A postal clerk earns a good salary.

_____ 3. There are mail carriers in every town in the United States.

_____ 4. A postal clerk is a person who sells stamps.

_____ 5. Postal clerks also deliver mail in a small truck.

_____ 6. Americans can apply for a passport at the post office.

_____ 7. It is expensive to insure a package.

_____ 8. All letters in the United States travel by plane.

_____ 9. People who have a post office box have to pick up their mail.

_____ 10. You need an airmail stamp if you are sending a letter from Texas to Michigan.

Skill Objectives: Learning about the U.S. Postal Service; reading for details. Read the introductory paragraphs aloud, then have the class reread them silently. Let students discuss the way their own mail is delivered. Ask students if they have ever been to the local post office. Where is it? Ask, "How much does it cost to mail a letter within the U.S.? How much does it cost to mail an airmail letter to your country?" Review the concept of the true/false/? type of exercise and discuss why the first two items are marked as they are. Then have students complete the page independently.

45

Do/Does/Don't/Doesn't

Use diagrams to help you choose the right form of do.

A. Use *do* and *does* to ask questions in the present tense. See the box below.

Do $\left.\begin{array}{l}\text{I}\\\text{you}\\\text{we}\\\text{they}\end{array}\right\}$ have the right change?   Does $\left.\begin{array}{l}\text{he}\\\text{she}\\\text{it}\end{array}\right\}$ work here?

Complete each sentence with *do* or *does*.

1. _____ you always have toast and coffee for breakfast?

2. _____ Ramon swim forty laps in the pool every day?

3. _____ David travel to many different countries on his job?

4. _____ nurses take care of patients in hospitals?

5. _____ you plan to become an electrician?

6. _____ your secretary always type so quickly?

7. _____ it snow in Hawaii?

8. _____ the Costellos always take their vacation in Miami?

B. Now look at this box.

$\left.\begin{array}{l}\text{I}\\\text{We}\\\text{You}\\\text{They}\end{array}\right\}$ don't have the time. $\left.\begin{array}{l}\text{He}\\\text{She}\\\text{It}\end{array}\right\}$ doesn't belong here.

Complete each sentence with *don't* or *doesn't*.

1. In an emergency, you _____ have to fill out forms.

2. I _____ know my account number.

3. The bank _____ pay a lot of interest on a regular savings account.

4. Many students _____ read newspapers at home.

5. We _____ eat turkey on Thanksgiving at our house.

6. Your last name _____ belong in this space.

7. We _____ like pizza very much.

8. Shaaren and Rajiv _____ like to clean the house.

Skill Objective: Simple present tense with *do/does*. *Part A:* Explain/review the uses of *do* and *does* in the box at the top. Do the first two items together before assigning Part A for independent work. *Part B:* Follow the same procedure as that for Part A.

Families

Here are the names of ten families:

The Clean Family   The Smart Family   The Happy Family   The Dirty Family
The Busy Family   The Quiet Family   The Tired Family   The Healthy Family
               The Angry Family   The Sad Family

Read each of the following paragraphs. Write the name of the family it is describing. The first one is done for you.

1. We never wash our hands or faces. We never wash our clothes, either. Our house is a mess, and our back yard is full of trash.   *The Dirty Family*

2. We always cry. We never smile. We never have a good time. Even Christmas and New Year's Day make us cry. _____

3. We never speak loudly. Everyone in our family whispers. We walk on tiptoe. Our dog, Silence, never barks. _____

4. Everyone in our family is a college graduate. We read the encyclopedia for fun. Grandpa knows the meaning of every word in the Oxford English Dictionary. _____

5. We eat lots of lean meat and fresh fruit and vegetables. We get lots of exercise. Everyone in this house gets a good night's sleep. We take our vitamins every day, too. _____

6. We sweep, we vacuum, we dust. There isn't any dirt in our house. Some of the people in this family take three showers a day. Even our cat gets a bath once a week. _____

7. Everyone in our family is a worker. We all have two jobs, or we go to work and to school. We don't have time to watch television or read a book. We all have things to do, places to go, and people to see. _____

8. Everyone in this family yawns all the time. We don't do too much. Father sometimes falls asleep when he drives the car, so you have to be careful when you're riding with him. Uncle Albert can never get up on time. _____

9. We fight like cats and dogs. Brother hates Sister, and Mother argues with Dad. We don't ever talk to any of our cousins. It's a terrible world; we hate it. _____

10. We take long rides in the country together. We love to play and joke with each other. Sometimes at night the whole family gets together to talk. All our friends say that they love to come to visit us. _____

Skill Objectives: Identifying topics; understanding characters' feelings. Read the names of the ten families aloud. Explain any unfamiliar adjectives. Ask a group of three students to come to the front of the class. Whisper the name of one of these families for the group to pantomime. The rest of the class must guess which family is being portrayed. Repeat this activity several times. Then assign the page for independent work.

47

A Future Job

Do you have a job now? Are you looking for a job? Do you know what kind of job you want? Finding a job is not always easy, but some jobs are easier to find than others. The list below shows about how many new workers are needed each year in various jobs in the United States.

A. **Look at the chart and use it to complete the sentences under it. Use your dictionary if you are not sure of some of the vocabulary.**

Jobs with the Most Openings

Occupation	Annual Openings	Occupation	Annual Openings
Secretaries & Stenographers	305,000	Blue-Collar Worker Supervisors	69,000
Cashiers	119,000	Local Truck Drivers	64,000
Bookkeeping Workers	96,000	Accountants	61,000
Nursing Aids, Orderlies and Attendants	94,000	Licensed Practical Nurses	60,000
Cooks and Chefs	86,000	Carpenters	58,000
Kindergarten and Elementary School Teachers	86,000	Real Estate Agents and Brokers	50,000
Registered Nurses	85,000	Construction Laborers	49,000
Waiters and Waitresses	70,000	Engineers	46,500
		Bank Clerks	45,000
		Private Household Workers	45,000

1. There are about _____305,000_____ openings for secretaries and stenographers each year.

2. There are about _____ openings for registered nurses and _____ openings for licensed practical nurses each year.

3. The total number of openings for construction workers and carpenters is about

    _____ .

4. The total number of openings for bookkeepers and accountants is _____ .

5. Public school systems don't need history teachers but they do need

    _____ and _____ teachers.

6. _____ need to know how to use a typewriter or a word processor.

7. _____ and _____ can help people and businesses keep track of their money.

8. Nurses work in hospitals. Other hospital jobs listed here are _____ ,

    _____ , and _____ .

B. Immigrants who come to the United States often do not speak much English when they arrive. **Name some jobs on the list that require little English.**

_____   _____   _____   _____

Skill Objectives: Learning about job openings in the U.S.; adding to find a total. Discuss jobs students have had and/or would like to have. Then discuss the chart, what it shows and what it does not show (it doesn't show how many people are employed in the occupations, for example, but only how many new openings there are each year). Explain new vocabulary. Have students read the numbers aloud. *Part A:* Do the first two items orally with the group, then assign for independent work. *Part B:* Discuss the question with the group and come to an agreement about which occupations to list.

What Are They Doing?

Read the information and choose an answer from the Data Bank to tell what each person is doing. The first one is done for you.

1. Bob is standing at home plate. He is swinging a bat and hitting a ball.

   What is he doing? *He's playing baseball.* _____

2. Paul and Joanne are mixing flour, eggs, butter, and sugar. They are turning on the oven.

   What are they doing? _____

3. Marco is sitting at his desk. He is holding a pen and writing on some paper. There is an envelope on the desk, too.

   What is he doing? _____

4. David is at the laundromat. He is putting detergent in one of the machines. He is putting coins into the slots.

   What is he doing? _____

5. Maria and her friends are listening to music. They are moving their feet, swinging their arms, and shaking their hair.

   What are they doing? _____

6. Paula Jenkins is walking from house to house. She is carrying a bag of letters, magazines, and newspapers.

   What is she doing? _____

7. The Nguyens are going to many different stores. They are looking at tables, chairs, sofas, bookcases, and bureaus.

   What are they doing? _____

8. The students are sitting at their desks quietly. Some are writing and some are erasing and changing their answers.

   What are they doing? _____

9. Betty is not eating any sugar or snacks. She is jogging every morning and riding her bicycle every afternoon.

   What is she doing? _____

10. Veronica is planning the menu. Jorge is renting the hall. Both of them are inviting the guests to the church and the reception.

    What are they doing? _____

D A T A   B A N K

dancing	**planning a wedding**	**buying furniture**	**making a cake**
trying to lose weight		**taking a test**	**delivering the mail**
playing baseball		**writing a letter**	**washing his clothes**

Skill Objectives: Drawing conclusions; reviewing the present progressive tense; building vocabulary. Do the first two or three items orally before assigning the page as independent work. Remind students that the answers are all in the Data Bank.

49

Helping You Study:
Using the Dictionary (2)

On page 38 you learned what part of the dictionary to find your word in. But you also need to know what page the word is on. To help you, the dictionary has guide words at the top of each page. These guide words are the first and last words on the page.

Look at the illustration at the right.
What is the first word on the page?

_____

What is the last word on the same page?

_____

Look at the sets of guide words below. Under each set of guide words are six other words. Decide which of these six words belong on the page with that set of guide words. If the word belongs on the page, write *yes*. If it does not belong on the page, write *no*.

BABY   BOTTLE
book _____
barn _____
break _____
battle _____
bill _____
best _____

LIGHT   LUCKY
lollipop _____
late _____
lend _____
lots _____
luck _____
like _____

SICK   STAY
socks _____
spend _____
see _____
stupid _____
stand _____
sell _____

QUART   QUORUM
quiet _____
quick _____
question _____
quack _____
quit _____
quote _____

CORN   CRUEL
crust _____
cruise _____
cove _____
cold _____
crab _____
cry _____

ECLIPSE   ENAMEL
eclair _____
educate _____
error _____
effect _____
end _____
entire _____

Skill Objective: Using guide words. Read the explanatory paragraph aloud. Let the class answer the guide word questions together. If possible, have students open dictionaries and note the use of guide words. Read the directions to the exercise, and do the first set or two as a group activity. If a word does *not* belong on the page, ask students if they would find it on the pages *before* or *after*. Assign the rest of the exercise as independent work. Correct the page together.

Dear Dot

Dear Dot—

My family is driving me crazy. I like to be the first person in the bathroom in the morning. I get up at 6:00 A.M., and I take my shower. Then I comb my hair, brush my teeth, put on my make-up, and give a little smile in the mirror—just to make sure I look okay. Before I finish, my father and mother are knocking at the door, and my brother and sister are yelling, "Hurry up!" Of course, this ruins the morning, and everyone is in a bad mood at breakfast. What can I do?

Maria

1. Who is driving Maria crazy? _____

2. When does Maria get up? _____

3. Why does Maria smile at the mirror? _____

   _____

4. What do her brother and sister yell? _____

5. Why is everyone in a bad mood at breakfast? _____

   _____

6. What does the word *yelling* in this letter mean? Circle the best answer.

   a. talking   b. playing   c. telling   d. screaming

7. What is your advice to Maria? Discuss with your classmates what she ought and ought not to do. Then play the part of Dot and write your answer to her.

   ___ *Dear Maria* ___ ,

   _____

   _____

   _____

   _____

   _____

   _____

   _____

Skill Objectives: Reading comprehension; understanding words through context; making judgments; writing a letter. Read the letter aloud or have a volunteer read it. Explain any unfamiliar words. Ask students to tell what "drives them crazy" or puts them in a bad mood. Have them reread the letter silently and answer questions 1-6. Correct these items. Then tell students that they are going to write Dot's answer to Maria. Have them discuss what their advice should be, then have them work independently to write their letters. Help them with letter format if necessary.

Vacation Plans

When we make plans for the future, we use *be going to* followed by the verb. See the examples in the box below.

PLANNING TO DO WHAT?		WHEN?
I *am going to go* to Hawaii.	We *are going to have* fun.	Next week
He *is going to swim*.	You *are going to relax*.	Tomorrow
She *is going to play* tennis.	They *are going to stay* at a hotel	In 3 days
It *is going to be* sunny.		Next winter.

A. Amy, Mike, Pam, and Lynn are making plans for their vacations. Use the travel ads at the top of the page to answer these questions about their plans.

1. Where is Amy going to go? _____

_____

2. How is she going to travel? _____

_____

3. Where is she going to stay? _____

_____

4. How long is she going to be there? _____

_____

5. What is she going to do there? _____

_____

6. How much is her vacation going to cost? _____

_____

(Go on to the next page.)

Skill Objectives: Future form: *going to*; reading travel ads; asking/answering questions. Have students look at the vacation ads and the box reviewing the "going to" structures. *Part A*: Call attention to Amy's plan to go to Hawaii, and ask the 6 questions. Have students answer orally in complete sentences, then write their sentences.

B. 1. Where are Pam and Lynn going to go? _____

_____

2. How are they going to get there? _____

_____

3. Where are they going to stay? _____

_____

4. How long are they going to be there? _____

_____

5. What are they going to do there? _____

_____

6. How much is their vacation going to cost? _____

_____

C. **On your paper, write questions and answers about Mike's vacation. Use the questions in Parts A and B as guides.**

D. **What about you? Imagine that you have just won $2000. Now you can take your dream vacation! On your paper, write answers to these questions about your dream vacation.**

1. Where are you going to go?
2. How are you going to get there?
3. When are you going to go?
4. What are you going to do or see?

5. How long are you going to stay?
6. Are you going to go with your family?
7. Are you going to stay at a hotel?
8. How much is your vacation going to cost?

E. **Now write about your dream vacation in paragraph form. Think of a good beginning sentence and a good ending sentence. Use more paper if you need to.**

_____

_____

_____

_____

_____

_____

_____

Skill Objectives: Asking/answering questions; writing a paragraph. *Part B:* Follow the same procedure as for Part A on the facing page, but this time do only sentence 1 orally. *Part C:* Have students write both the questions and the answers for Mike. Use the same six questions but with the pronoun "he." *Part D:* Discuss these questions, then have students write their answers on separate paper. *Part E:* Have them use their answers from Part D as a source for their paragraph-form description. Discuss the idea of having their first sentence be a topic sentence and their last sentence be a summary.

53

The Festival of San Fermin

Every year, people from all over Europe and North and South America travel to Pamplona. They go to this city in Northern Spain because every summer, during the week of July 7th, there is a seven-day celebration called the Festival of San Fermin.

During the week there are parties and parades and bullfights. Everyone is happy and friendly. Some people try to stay awake during the whole week because, day or night, there is always something going on or some new friends to meet in the town.

The most exciting part of the festival is the "running of the bulls." Every morning at 6:00, men (and a few women) stand in the middle of a special street. At one end of the street is a bull pen, where six angry bulls are standing, waiting to be free. At the other end of the street is the arena where, later in the day, the bullfights are going to happen. When the bells ring at 6:00, someone shoots a gun and the bulls can leave their pen. They run after the people standing in the streets. The people run in front of the bulls into the arena. If the people make it into the arena, they jump behind a wall where the bulls cannot hurt them.

Every year someone in the street gets hurt. Sometimes, someone is killed. Still the people come back. The excitement of the race and the fun of the week bring them back every year.

A. Read the story. Then answer these questions. The first one is done for you.

1. Where is Pamplona? _____ *It's in Northern Spain.* _____

2. What is the Festival of San Fermin? _____

   _____

3. What happens during the Festival of San Fermin? _____

   _____

4. Why do some people try not to sleep during the festival? _____

   _____

5. What is the most exciting part of the festival? _____

   _____

6. Where do the bulls and people run to? _____

7. What happens every year to someone in the street? _____

   _____

8. Why do people come back? _____

B. What is the story mostly about? Circle the best answer.

a. a visit to Spain   c. the return of the people

b. the city of Pamplona   d. the running of the bulls

Skill Objective: Identifying main idea and details. Read the story aloud. Explain any unfamiliar vocabulary. Help students locate Spain, then the city of Pamplona on a map. Ask students to reread the story, then complete Parts A and B independently. Correct as a class. Make sure students understand why choice d is the best answer to Part B. Ask students if they would like to go to Pamplona and take part in the "running of the bulls." Why or why not? Encourage lively discussion.

Choose the Right Word

Complete each sentence with one of the following words or pairs of words: *in, on, at, to, from, next to, before, after.* The first one is done for you.

1. Pedro is ___from___ Cuba.

2. She always goes to the supermarket _____ Friday.

3. Bill went to the movies _____ nine o'clock.

4. Sue and Jan went for a walk _____ the park.

5. Mary is writing a letter _____ her mother.

6. Always wash your hands _____ you eat.

7. What time do you get up _____ the morning?

8. The Jones family lives _____ the Smith family.

9. We go _____ the movies every Saturday.

10. Bob is waiting _____ the bus stop.

11. She is going to Puerto Rico _____ July.

12. November comes _____ October.

13. Harry works _____ the office _____ the first floor.

14. John likes to sit _____ me at lunch.

15. The bank is _____ the corner of Dudley St. and Columbia Road.

16. It's raining _____ Miami today.

17. We get letters _____ John every week.

18. Betty is talking _____ the teacher.

19. He is looking _____ the pictures in the museum.

20. October always comes _____ November.

21. Monday always comes _____ Sunday.

22. Where is he _____?

23. Please sit _____ the red chair.

24. What does Fred do _____ Monday?

What Are They Going to Do?

Each of these people has a problem. What is he or she going to do? Write an answer for each problem.

1. Mr. Gonzales leaves his house. His car has a flat tire. He has to get to work soon. What is he going to do?

    _____

    _____

2. Laura comes home late from work. Her house is a mess. The beds aren't made, and there are dirty dishes in the sink. Friends are coming over to visit in thirty minutes. What is she going to do?

    _____

    _____

3. Paul has a problem. He doesn't have his front door key. His parents are out visiting friends. His brother has a key, but Paul can't find him. What is Paul going to do?

    _____

    _____

4. The Wongs live in a very small five-room apartment. There are eight people in the Wong family. They need more space to live in. They don't like their apartment any more. What are they going to do?

    _____

    _____

5. Rosa is sick. This is the third day that she has to stay in bed. She is taking aspirin. She is drinking lots of liquid, but she isn't feeling any better. What is she going to do?

    _____

    _____

(Go on to the next page.)

Skill Objectives: Making predictions; creative problem solving. This page and the following present a number of creative problem-solving situations. Both pages can be effectively used in oral group activity. Read each situation aloud. Explain unfamiliar words. Encourage students to suggest as many different solutions as possible. As an incentive, keep a tally of the number of solutions offered for each situation. After all ten items have been discussed, assign the pages for independent work. Students should choose one solution to write after each problem.

56

6. Deborah walks into her apartment. It is freezing. She turns on the heat, but nothing happens. Deborah goes downstairs to the basement. Something is wrong with the furnace. There is no heat in the house. What is she going to do?

_____

_____

7. Vinh is at a school dance. He sees a beautiful girl across the room. She sees him. They smile at each other. The band begins to play a slow song. Vinh walks over to her. What is he going to do?

_____

_____

8. Margarita gets a headache when she reads for a long time. She can't see objects that are far away. Sometimes her eyes hurt her. What is she going to do?

_____

_____

9. Mr.Lee is the boss at the Olson factory. Jack, one of his workers, is almost always late. Many other days Jack calls in sick or leaves work early. Today he is two hours late. What is Mr. Lee going to do?

_____

_____

10. The baby is crying. The dog is barking. Cars and trucks are passing by and making noises. Mr. Mleczko is watching the news on TV. He can't hear a thing. What is he going to do?

_____

_____

Skill Objectives: Making predictions; creative problem solving. See annotation on page 56.

57

In, On, Under

Where can you find each of the sets of things on the left? The column at the right has the answers. Write the letter of the right answer in the blank for each set of things. Use each answer only once. The first one is done for you.

_q_   1. stars, sun, moon

____   2. principal, teachers, students

____   3. candles, frosting, icing

____   4. Empire State Building, Broadway, Statue of Liberty

____   5. milk, butter, cheese

____   6. cows, chickens, barn

____   7. sofa, television, armchair

____   8. dust, shoes, slippers

____   9. Spain, France, England

____ 10. pictures, posters, light-switch

____ 11. sailors, cabins, deck

____ 12. shower, sink, toilet

____ 13. lions, tigers, elephants

____ 14. traffic, subway, buildings

____ 15. nose, eyes, mouth

____ 16. shells, shipwrecks, cables

____ 17. coats, hats, dresses

____ 18. flowers, tomatoes, corn

____ 19. pots, pans, kettle

____ 20. bones, blood, heart

____ 21. players, goal posts, soccer ball

____ 22. apples, bananas, oranges

____ 23. subway, pipes, wires

____ 24. Hawaii, Japan, the Philippines

____ 25. pickles, peanut butter, jelly

____ 26. tables, waiters, menus

a. in a living room

b. on a field

c. in the Pacific Ocean

d. on a boat

e. on a wall

f. on a face

g. on trees

h. under the ground

i. in a restaurant

j. in a school

k. under the sea

l. in the refrigerator

m. in a garden

n. on a farm

o. in a closet

p. on a cake

q. in the sky

r. in a city

s. in a zoo

t. on a stove

u. under the skin

v. in jars

w. in the bathroom

x. in Europe

y. under the bed

z. in New York City

Menu

Skill Objectives: Using prepositional phrases; classifying. Do several items as an oral group exercise, then assign the page as independent written work. To correct, have students cover the right hand column and try to recall the prepositional phrase as you ask, "Where can you find . . .?"

Early Morning

Mrs. Olsen is a teacher at the Parkman School. She arrives at school at 7:00. She goes to the teachers' room, and she has coffee with her friends, Mr. Stanton, the history teacher, and Mrs. Fung, the math teacher. At 7:15, Mrs. Olsen leaves the teachers' room. She goes upstairs to her classroom. She sits at her desk and begins to work.

Mrs. Olsen corrects some tests. She prepares her lessons for today's classes. At 7:45, she gets up from her desk. Mrs. Olsen writes some exercises on the chalkboard. At 8:00, the first bell rings. Her students enter the classroom. Mrs. Olsen smiles at the students and says hello. At 8:05, the second bell rings. Mrs. Olsen begins to teach.

A. Read the story. Then answer these questions. Use short answers.

1. Where does Mrs. Olsen teach? _____

2. Who are Mrs. Olsen's friends? _____

3. When do the students enter the classroom? _____

4. When does Mrs. Olsen begin to teach? _____

B. Which of the following statements is most likely true about Mrs. Olsen? Circle your answer.

a. She is a mean, unfriendly person.

b. She is the principal of the Parkman School.

c. She likes teaching at the Parkman School.

d. She teaches history and math.

C. Put numbers on the line before each statement to show the correct order. The number 1 is done for you.

_____ She sits at her desk.

_____ The first bell rings.

_____ She corrects some tests.

_____ She has coffee with her friends.

_____ The students enter the room.

_____ She prepares her lessons.

_1_ She arrives at school.

_____ The second bell rings.

_____ She goes upstairs to her classroom.

_____ She writes some exercises on the board.

Skill Objectives: Identifying main idea and details; making inferences; sequencing. Read the story aloud. Explain any unfamiliar words. Have students reread the story before answering the comprehension questions independently. Correct and discuss the answers as a class.

59

Helping You Study:
Alphabetical Order (3)

A. When you alphabetize people's names, you put the last name first, then the first name and middle name or initial (if it is given). **Rewrite these famous names this way. Then write them in alphabetical order.** The first line in each column is done for you.

	Rewrite	Alphabetize
Thomas Edison	*Edison, Thomas*	*Alcott, Louisa May*
Christopher Columbus		
Harriet Beecher Stowe		
George Washington		
Louisa May Alcott		
Susan B. Anthony		
Katherine Hepburn		
Alexander Graham Bell		
Neil Armstrong		
Nancy Lopez		

B. After your teacher corrects your work, or you are sure that you are correct, do these names the same way.

Noah Webster		
Harriet Tubman		
Stephen Austin		
Henry Aaron		
Annie Oakley		
Jonas Salk		
Eleanor Roosevelt		
Helen Keller		
Amelia Earhart		
Jesse James		

Skill Objective: Listing people alphabetically by last names. Write several student names on the board. Ask the class how you would find a certain student's number in the phone book. Establish that last names are listed alphabetically. As a group, rewrite the students' names, last name first, then alphabetize the list. Assign the page as independent work. Extension Activities: 1) How many of the listed names can the class identify? 2) Help students draw up an alphabetized class directory with addresses and phone numbers.

Dear Dot

Dear Dot—

My family moves around a lot. Every year I go to a different school. Sometimes the work is boring, because I know all the subjects already. Other times, the work is all new to me, and I don't understand it. This year I like my school a lot. The work is interesting, and I have many friends. Now my mother says we are going to leave this town and go to another state. I don't want to leave. What can I do?

Happy Where I Am

1. Why does Happy go to so many different schools? _____

_____

2. Why is school boring for Happy sometimes? _____

_____

3. Why is it too difficult other times? _____

_____

4. What did Happy's mother tell him? _____

_____

5. How does Happy feel about the news? _____

_____

6. What does the word *boring* in this letter mean? Circle the best answer.

   a. difficult   b. lively   c. fascinating   d. uninteresting

7. Talk with your classmates about what Happy should do. Then write your answer to him.

   Dear Happy Where I Am ,
   _____

   _____

   _____

   _____

   _____

   _____

   _____

                                                    _____

Skill Objectives: Reading comprehension; understanding words through context; making judgments; writing a letter. Read the letter aloud or have a volunteer read it. Explain any unfamiliar words. Ask students to reread the letter silently and answer questions 1-6. Correct these items. Then have the students discuss what their advice to Happy would be; finally have them write Dot's answer, incorporating this advice.

Only Joking

A riddle is a question with a silly or unexpected answer. Here are some riddles. The answers are in the column at the right. **Write the letter of the correct answer in the blank in front of the riddle.** The first one is done for you.

_g_ 1. Why do birds fly south for the winter?

____ 2. What never asks questions but gets lots of answers?

____ 3. Ten people are walking under one small umbrella. They aren't getting wet. Why not?

____ 4. How can you spell "mousetrap" in three letters?

____ 5. How can you keep a fish from smelling?

____ 6. What has a neck but no head?

____ 7. What kind of dress do you have but don't wear?

____ 8. What comes once in a minute, once in a month, but never in a thousand years?

____ 9. What do you take off last before you go to bed?

____ 10. What is everyone in the world doing at the same time?

____ 11. What has one eye open but cannot see?

____ 12. What has four legs, a back, and two arms but cannot move?

____ 13. If a woman is born in Spain, grows up in Japan, and dies in the U.S., what is she?

____ 14. What always smiles and frowns when you do, but parts its hair on the other side?

____ 15. What is the longest word in the English language?

a. the letter "m"

b. a chair

c. your mirror image

d. your address

e. your feet on the floor

f. Cut off its nose.

g. It's too far to walk.

h. the doorbell

i. a bottle

j. getting older

k. dead

l. a needle

m. smiles (There's a mile between the two s's.)

n. C-A-T

o. It isn't raining.

Skill Objective: Understanding riddles. Solve the first few riddles as a group, then let students complete the page independently or in pairs. Extension Activities: 1) Help students locate the joke and riddle books, if any, in their school library. 2) Plan a time for students to tell new jokes and riddles to their classmates. 3) Establish a corner of the bulletin board where students can post favorite comic strips from the newspaper or jokes and riddles they have read or heard.

The Simple Past Tense

The simple past tense is used to talk about activities or situations that began or ended in the past, for example, "Bob stayed home yesterday," "It rained all night long." Most simple past tense verbs are formed by adding *-ed* to the verb.

Forms of the Simple Past

Statement: I (you/he/she/it/we/they) worked yesterday.

Question: Did I (you/he/she/it/we/they) work yesterday?

Write a sentence under each picture. Use the correct past tense verb from the Data Bank. (One of the words is used twice.) The first one is done for you.

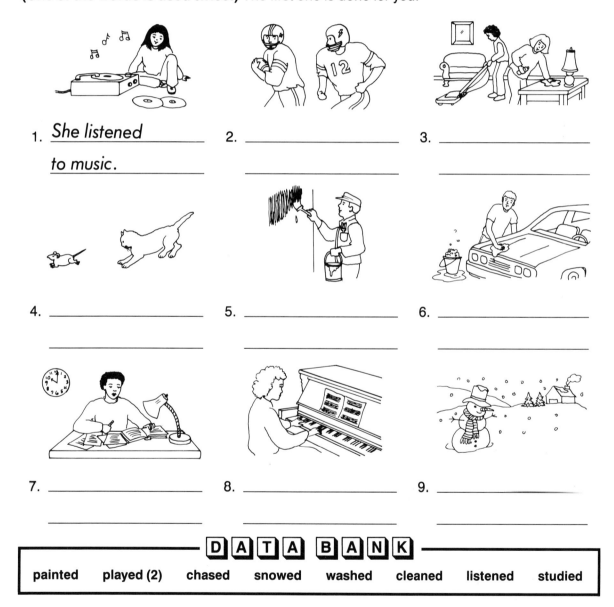

1. *She listened to music.*

2. _____

3. _____

4. _____

5. _____

6. _____

7. _____

8. _____

9. _____

DATA BANK

painted   played (2)   chased   snowed   washed   cleaned   listened   studied

Skill Objectives: Forming past tense of regular verbs; writing sentences. Write on the board, "What did you do yesterday?" Ask individual students such questions as, "Did you watch TV? What programs did you *see*?" "Did you listen to music?" etc. Read the explanation of the simple past tense and the forms of the simple past. Have the class look at Item 1. Explain that in each item, *ed* is added to the verb to form the simple past. Call attention to the Data Bank, then do the nine items orally before having students write the sentences.

What Did They Do?

To change most verbs to the past tense, add *ed*. If the verb ends in *e*, just add *d*.

walk—Yesterday, they walked.   **bike**—Last Monday, they biked.

The *ed* ending can stand for three different sounds, "d," "t," and "id." **Say the sentence for each picture. Then write the verb on the line.** The first one is done for you.

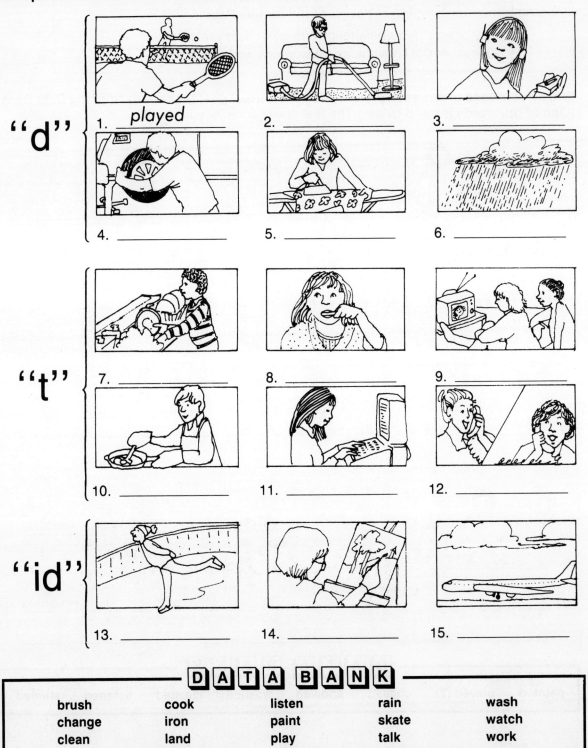

"d"
1. played
2. _____
3. _____
4. _____
5. _____
6. _____

"t"
7. _____
8. _____
9. _____
10. _____
11. _____
12. _____

"id"
13. _____
14. _____
15. _____

DATA BANK

brush	cook	listen	rain	wash
change	iron	paint	skate	watch
clean	land	play	talk	work

Skill Objectives: Forming simple past tense; pronunciation of final -ed. Review the rule and examples. Work with the first block of pictures: -ed as "d." Say a sentence for each picture: "Yesterday she ironed her blouse." Have students identify the picture and repeat the sentence. Repeat with the other two blocks of pictures. Next, have each student question the person on his/her left. *Student A:* "Number (9) What did they do yesterday?" *Student B:* "They watched TV. (to Student C) Number 6. What did it do yesterday?" Correct students' pronunciation. Assign page for written work.

64

How Does It Sound?

Your teacher will read you each of the verbs in the box. Listen to the ending sound of each verb. Some of the verbs end with a *d* sound. Some of them end with a *t* sound. Some of them end with the sound of *id*. **As your teacher reads each of the verbs, decide which sound it ends with, and write it in the correct column under the box.** The first three are done for you.

ironed	closed	cleaned
painted	wanted	washed
polished	watched	baked
played	delivered	hated
kissed	brushed	traveled
typed	rented	planted
corrected	waited	parked
changed	arrived	called
worked	tasted	landed
fixed	opened	dated

"d"

1. *ironed*
2. _____
3. _____
4. _____
5. _____
6. _____
7. _____
8. _____
9. _____
10. _____

"t"

1. *polished*
2. _____
3. _____
4. _____
5. _____
6. _____
7. _____
8. _____
9. _____
10. _____

"id"

1. *painted*
2. _____
3. _____
4. _____
5. _____
6. _____
7. _____
8. _____
9. _____
10. _____

Skill Objectives: Simple past tense; distinguishing among the three sounds of -ed. Pronounce each verb. Have students repeat, paying particular attention to the final -ed sound. As a group, decide in which column the word belongs. Allow time for writing. Extension Activity: Have students use the past tense verbs in original oral sentences.

Adding "ed"

There are some important spelling rules to know when you add *ed* to form the past tense. (These rules work for most words, but there are exceptions.)

Rule 1: For most words, add *ed* with no change. Examples: *paint, painted; rent, rented.*

Rule 2: For words that end in *e*, drop the *e* and add *ed*. Examples: *type, typed; close, closed.*

Rule 3: For words that end in a consonant + *y*, change *y* to *i* and add *ed*. Examples: *hurry, hurried; marry, married.*

Rule 4: For one-syllable words that end in consonant + vowel + consonant (except *w, x, y*), double the final letter and add *ed*. Examples: *rob, robbed; bag, bagged.*

A. Now use these rules to add *ed* to the following words.

1. serve _____	16. design _____	31. cash _____
2. ask _____	17. direct _____	32. install _____
3. try _____	18. announce _____	33. talk _____
4. love _____	19. stop _____	34. practice _____
5. arrest _____	20. live _____	35. play _____
6. stay _____	21. match _____	36. empty _____
7. rain _____	22. clean _____	37. end _____
8. lift _____	23. bark _____	38. listen _____
9. study _____	24. help _____	39. yawn _____
10. cook _____	25. carry _____	40. hope _____
11. chase _____	26. dance _____	41. pass _____
12. like _____	27. learn _____	42. mix _____
13. show _____	28. smile _____	43. use _____
14. push _____	29. repair _____	44. cry _____
15. move _____	30. snow _____	45. visit _____

B. On another sheet of paper, write sentences for 15 of the past tense *(ed)* words you wrote above. Use words such as *yesterday, last week,* and *ago* to show the past tense.

Skill Objective: Forming simple past tense, observing spelling changes. Go over the four rules at the top of the page; elicit additional examples. *Part A:* Complete the first several items as a class, having volunteers write the correct past tense form on the board. Then assign Part A as independent work. *Part B:* Ask volunteers to make up sample sentences using the first three or four verbs and including cue words (*yesterday,* etc) to emphasize that the sentence refers to something in the past. Then have students write their fifteen (or more if they wish) sentences. You may wish to have each student read his/her favorite sentence aloud.

66

A Time Line

A time line gives information in chronological order, that is, the order in which it happened. It shows what things happened at different times. Read this time line from left to right. It shows some things that happened to one man from 1981 through 1990.

TEN YEARS OF RICK SUMMERS'S LIFE

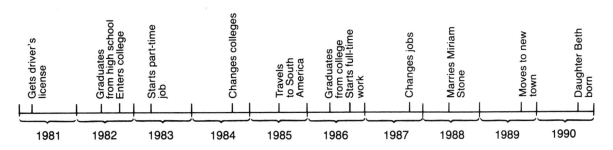

A. Use the time line to answer these questions. Write *Yes, he did,* or *No, he didn't.*

1. Did Rick travel to South America in 1983? _____

2. Did Rick get his driver's license in 1981? _____

3. Did Rick start his full-time job in 1988? _____

4. Did Rick enter college in 1984? _____

5. Did Rick marry Miriam in 1985? _____

6. Did Rick graduate from college in 1982? _____

7. Did Rick change colleges in 1984? _____

8. Did Rick graduate from high school in 1982? _____

9. Did Rick start his part-time job in 1983? _____

10. Did Rick move to a new town in 1989? _____

11. Did Rick and Miriam have a daughter in 1989? _____

12. Did Rick change jobs in 1986? _____

B. What about you? Fill in this time line for yourself. Put in important events in your own life. List the years below the line. Be sure to include ALL the years between the first one you list and the last one.

19

Skill Objective: Interpreting and charting a time line. Examine the time line with the students. Read the dates and events aloud together. Explain any unfamiliar words. Answer the first few questions as a group activity. Make sure students understand how to use the chart to locate information, then assign the page for independent work. Provide help with Part B as needed. Extension Activity: Have students form pairs and ask their partner questions about his/her time line: "Did you . . . (move to Virginia) in 1982?"

It's a Record!

A. Before you read the story, look at the Vocabulary Preview. Be sure that you know
the meaning of each word. Use the dictionary. Some words have more than one
meaning. The way the word is used in the story will help you decide the meaning
you want. Write down the meanings of the words you are not sure of.

Vocabulary Preview

unusual	huge
incredible	dessert
sneeze	legally
record	divorce
omelet	fascinating

B. Now read the story. Use the dictionary if there are other words that you are not sure
of. Notice that the words from the Vocabulary Preview are underlined.

The People of the
Guinness Book of World Records

To get into the *Guinness Book of World Records* you have to be an unusual person or you have to do something incredible. Jon Brower Minnoch is in the book because he weighed 1,400 pounds. ZengJinlian is in the book because she was 8 ft. 3¼ in. tall. A woman from Russia, Mrs. Feodor Vassiliev, is in the book because she had 69 children. Donna Griffiths sneezed for 978 days. Of course she is in the book too. These are just some of the unusual people in the *Guinness Book of World Records*.

What incredible things do people do to get into the record book? Lorenzo Amato baked a pizza that weighed 18,664 pounds. Michael McGowan of Las Vegas, Nevada, cooked an omelet to get into the book. He used 54,763 eggs to make his record breaking breakfast.

Some students at Princeton University wanted to get into the book. They decided to make a four-mile-long banana split. They used tons of bananas, thousands of gallons of ice cream, and hundreds of pounds of nuts for this huge dessert.

Mr. Glynn Wolfe from the United States also did something amazing to get into the Guinness book. He legally married and divorced 27 women—more than any other man in the Western world. Mrs. Beverly Nina Avery holds the record for women. She married and divorced 16 different men. The *Guinness Book of World Records* has many other interesting and unusual facts. Some records change from year to year. Look in your bookstore or library and read this fascinating book.

(Go on to the next page.)

Skill Objectives: Reading comprehension; building vocabulary; using simple past tense. Allow time for students to look up vocabulary
words in the dictionary and choose the appropriate definitions. Review the definitions together. If you wish, read the selection aloud before asking
students to read it silently.

68

C. Use a word from the Vocabulary Preview to complete each of these sentences.

1. Tommy is allergic to cats; they make him _____ .

2. Don't each too much! There is chocolate cake for _____ .

3. We listened to every word the professor said. His lecture was _____ .

4. No one believed the size of the professional football players; they were _____ .

5. This store is never crowded. It's _____ to see so many people here.

D. Now answer these questions. Use complete sentences. The first one is done for you.

1. How much did John Brower Minnoch weigh? *He weighed 1,400 pounds.*

2. How many children did Mrs. Vassiliev have? _____
   _____

3. How many days did Donna Griffiths sneeze for? _____
   _____

4. What did Lorenzo Amato do to get into the Guinness book? _____
   _____

5. What did Michael McGowan do to get into the book? _____
   _____

6. How many eggs did he use? _____

7. What did the students at Princeton decide to make? _____
   _____

8. How much ice cream did they use? _____

9. How many women did Mr. Wolfe marry? _____

10. How many men did Mrs. Beverly Nina Avery marry? _____
    _____

Skill Objectives: Reading comprehension; building vocabulary; using simple past tense. Students should complete the exercises independently. Expansion Activities: Help students locate other collections of strange and unusual facts in the library. If your newspaper carries a column or fillers about unusual records, have students collect and share the clippings. Encourage students to report strange bits of knowledge to the class, then pose their facts in a "That's Incredible!" display.

Helping You Study: Using the Encyclopedia

You use the dictionary to look up the meaning of a word. If you want more information, you can look in an encyclopedia. Encyclopedias give information about people, places, things, events, and ideas.

The information in the encyclopedia, like the information in the dictionary, is in alphabetical order. Because encyclopedias contain more information about a subject than dictionaries do, most of them have several books or volumes. The letters on the outside of each volume tell you which words are in

that volume. They usually are the first few letters of the first and last words in the volume.

Look at the encyclopedia below. Notice that there are 30 volumes. Each volume has a number on it, as well as the letters that tell what words are in it. Write the number of the volume in which you can look for information about each of the people on the list. Remember that people are always listed by their last name. The first one is done for you.

1	2	3	4	5	6	7	8	9	10	11	12	13	14	15
A–ANN	ANN–BAC	BAD–BYZ	C–CUP	CUR–DEM	DEN–DYS	E–ENG	ENH–EYR	F–FLY	FO–GRA	GRE–HEY	HI–JOB	JOC–LED	LEE–KRA	KRE–LYT

16	17	18	19	20	21	22	23	24	25	26	27	28	29	30
M–MON	MOO–NAZ	NE–NYX	O–ORC	ORD–PUN	PUP–QUA	QUE–RAB	RAC–RY	S–SOT	SOU–SYZ	T–TOX	TOY–UMA	UMB–VIB	VIC–WYZ	X–Y–Z

Write the number of the book where you find:

Thomas Edison ___7___

Christopher Columbus _____

Harriet Beecher Stowe _____

George Washington _____

Louisa May Alcott _____

Susan B. Anthony _____

Alexander Graham Bell _____

Neil Armstrong _____

Orville and Wilbur Wright _____

Noah Webster _____

Harriet Tubman _____

Stephen Austin _____

John Quincy Adams _____

Annie Oakley _____

Jonas Salk _____

Eleanor Roosevelt _____

Helen Keller _____

Amelia Earhart _____

Skill Objectives: Selecting the correct encyclopedia volume; alphabetizing. Read and discuss the explanatory paragraphs with the class. Locate the first few names as a group activity, then assign the page for independent work. Extension Activities: 1) Help students locate the encyclopedias in the school library and identify which are the most simply written. 2) If your encyclopedia has an index, show students how it can be used. 3) Let each student choose one name from the list on this page to look up in the school encyclopedia.

70

When Did It Happen?

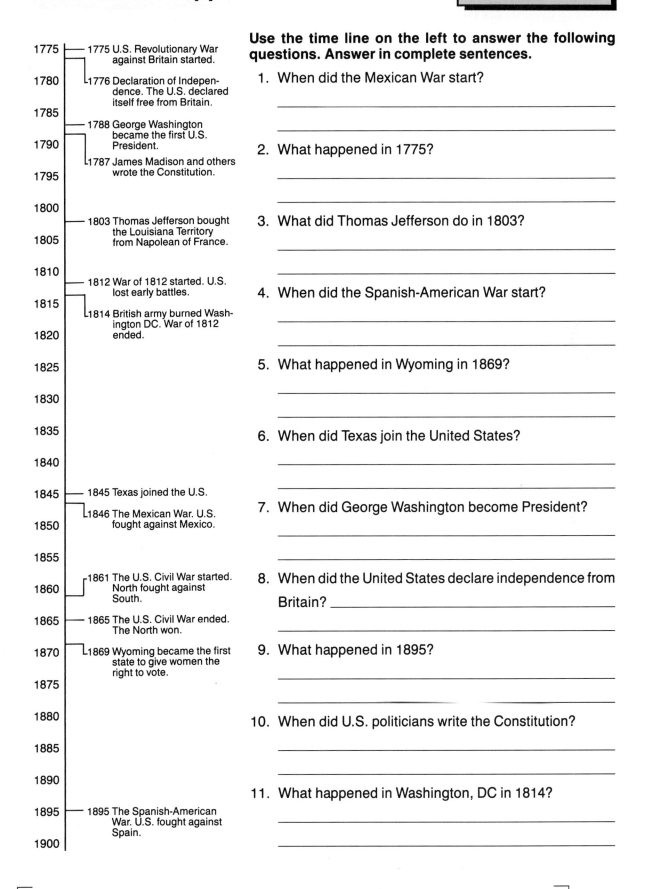

1775 — 1775 U.S. Revolutionary War against Britain started.

1780 └1776 Declaration of Independence. The U.S. declared itself free from Britain.

1785

— 1788 George Washington became the first U.S. President.

1790

└1787 James Madison and others wrote the Constitution.

1795

1800

— 1803 Thomas Jefferson bought the Louisiana Territory from Napolean of France.

1805

1810

— 1812 War of 1812 started. U.S. lost early battles.

1815

└1814 British army burned Washington DC. War of 1812 ended.

1820

1825

1830

1835

1840

1845 — 1845 Texas joined the U.S.

└1846 The Mexican War. U.S. fought against Mexico.

1850

1855

1860 ┌1861 The U.S. Civil War started. North fought against South.

1865 — 1865 The U.S. Civil War ended. The North won.

1870 └1869 Wyoming became the first state to give women the right to vote.

1875

1880

1885

1890

1895 — 1895 The Spanish-American War. U.S. fought against Spain.

1900

Use the time line on the left to answer the following questions. Answer in complete sentences.

1. When did the Mexican War start?

_____

_____

2. What happened in 1775?

_____

_____

3. What did Thomas Jefferson do in 1803?

_____

_____

4. When did the Spanish-American War start?

_____

_____

5. What happened in Wyoming in 1869?

_____

_____

6. When did Texas join the United States?

_____

_____

7. When did George Washington become President?

_____

_____

8. When did the United States declare independence from Britain? _____

_____

9. What happened in 1895?

_____

_____

10. When did U.S. politicians write the Constitution?

_____

_____

11. What happened in Washington, DC in 1814?

_____

_____

Skill Objectives: Interpreting a time line; sequencing. Have volunteers read the notations on the time line aloud. Provide help with reading dates and with vocabulary if necessary. Then go through the eleven questions orally, having students answer in complete sentences. If students have additional knowledge about any of the events or places, encourage discussion. Have students complete the page independently, writing their answers in complete sentences.

Dear Dot

Make judgments and draw conclusions to write an answer to a letter.

Dear Dot—

    Yesterday I didn't have to go to work. I cleaned my room and my roommate's room too. I waxed the floor and emptied the baskets. I shortened one of my skirts and one of hers too. I cooked dinner, but Anna's burned by mistake. Now Anna is mad at me. Can you believe it? After I did all those things for her, she's mad at me. What can I do?

                               Jane

1. What did Jane do yesterday? _____

_____

2. Why do you think Anna is mad at Jane? _____

_____

3. Is Anna right to be mad at Jane? Why or why not? _____

_____

4. What does the word *mad* mean in this letter? Circle the best answer.

    a. happy   b. sad   c. angry   d. surprised

5. Write a letter to Jane. Tell her what you think she ought to do.

_Dear Jane_____ ,

_____

_____

_____

_____

_____

_____

_____

                                                _____

Skill Objectives: Reading comprehension; understanding words through context; making judgments; writing a letter. Have a volunteer read the letter aloud while the class follows along. Explain any unfamiliar vocabulary. Ask students to reread the letter silently and answer questions 1–4. Discuss their answers to questions 2 and 3. Then talk about what their advice to Jane would be, and have them take Dear Dot's role and write their replies.

Irregular Past Tense

Some verbs have irregular past forms. Look at the following examples.

I **had** a bad dream last night. Sue **went** to Germany last year.
They **ate** lunch at school yesterday. Tran **rang** the doorbell but no one answered.

A. **Use the Data Bank to find the correct irregular past tense verb for each picture. Write a sentence about the picture using that verb.** The first one is done for you.

1. *She broke her leg.*

2. _____

3. _____

4. _____

5. _____

6. _____

7. _____

8. _____

9. _____

D A T A   B A N K

break — broke	go — went (shopping)	write — wrote	sleep — slept
take — took	hurt — hurt	eat — ate	run — ran
see — saw	do —did (exercises)	have — had	ring — rang

B. **Use the correct form of the verb from the Data Bank to complete the sentences. Use the past tense form.**

1. I can't believe that Marisa _____ five sandwiches for lunch.

2. A few days ago I _____ a good movie.

3. Tom _____ a bad headache yesterday.

4. Ann and Susan _____ the bus to class yesterday.

What's the Problem?

Solve the following problems. The first one is done for you.

Your Answer

1. Mr. Thompson was on vacation. He played six games of tennis every day for a week. How many games of tennis did he play?

____42____ games

2. Peter didn't do well on his history test. He got only 30 questions right out of 50. What per cent of the questions did Peter get right?

_____ %

3. Yesterday, Diana read 90 pages of her new book. Her book has 270 pages. What fraction of the book did Diana read yesterday?

_____

4. Mrs. Lee baked a cake yesterday. She used 2½ cups of flour, 1¼ cups of white sugar, and ¼ cup of butter. How many cups of ingredients did she use altogether?

_____ cups

5. Bill worked on his checkbook yesterday. He had $500.48, but he had to pay four bills: $89.50, $85.02, $66.10, and $25.40. How much did he have after he paid the bills?

_____

6. Roberto wanted to know his grade for the second term. He needed to find out the average of his tests. His marks were 96, 91, 80, and 61. What is the average of his four tests?

_____

7. Six people had dinner in a restaurant. The total bill was $96.12. How much did each person have to pay if the six people shared the bill evenly?

_____

8. Maria's American friend, Joanne, asked how much Maria weighed. "Fifty kilograms," answered Maria. Joanne didn't know that a kilogram equals 2.2 pounds. How much does Maria weigh in pounds?

_____ pounds

9. An express train left Charlestown at 3:00. It arrived at Centerville at 8:00. The train traveled 50 mph for the entire trip. How far is Charlestown from Centerville?

_____ miles

10. What is the odd number that is less than 60 but more than 50 and is divisible by 11 and 5?

_____

11. A factor is a number that can be divided evenly into another number. List all the factors of 50 including 1 and 50.

12. A square root is a number which multiplied by itself gives another number. 4 is the square root of 16 (4 x 4 = 16). What is the square root of 64?

_____

Skill Objective: Solving mathematical word problems. Read the first problem aloud. Ask, "What do we want to find out? What facts do we know?" List the facts on the board: *6 games every day. Played 7 days.* Let students discuss what process should be used to solve the problem, then write the mathematical equation: 6 x 7 = _____ . Do the first three word problems as a group. Students who are comfortable with the skill can then complete the page independently. Continue to work closely with other students. Answers can be found on page 125.

The Present and Past of "To Be"

Present	Past
I am happy.	I was happy.
She is sick.	She was sick.
He is a student.	He was a student.
It is sunny.	It was sunny.
You are tired.	You were tired.
We are late for class.	We were late for class.
They are in the kitchen.	They were in the kitchen.

A. Look at the chart below. Then write sentences about each person. Use the past and present forms of the verb "to be." The first one is done for you.

Person	Past Job	Years	Present Job
1. Susan	secretary	1967–1973	travel agent
2. David	football player	1974–1983	businessman
3. Tom and Amy	cashiers	1982–1986	store managers
4. Kate	teacher	1963–1974	computer programmer
5. Jose	salesman	1984–1987	disc jockey

1. *Susan was a secretary for six years. Now she is a travel agent.*

2. _____

3. _____

4. _____

5. _____

B. Answer these questions with short sentences. The first one is done for you.

1. Is Texas a state? *Yes, it is.*

2. Were you in class yesterday? _____

3. Are you from China? _____

4. Was your teacher sick yesterday? _____

5. Was it sunny on Saturday? _____

6. Is your mother a doctor? _____

7. Are Boston and Miami states? _____

8. Were the streets wet this morning? _____

Skill Objectives: Past tense of *to be*; comparing uses of the present and past tense. Teach/review the present and past forms of "to be." *Part A:* Go through this as an oral group exercise before assigning it as written work. *Part B:* Do the first two items together, then have the students complete Part B independently.

75

Sally Ride

A. Read the biography of Sally Ride, first American woman astronaut. Then write questions about her. The answer to each question is at the right. The question you write has to go with this answer. The first word of each question is at the left. The first question is done for you.

1951	Was born in California
1969	Graduated from high school
1973	Received 2 Bachelor's Degrees (B.S. and B.A.) from Stanford University
1976	Got a Ph.D. in Physics
1977	Applied to be an astronaut
1978	Began astronaut training
1980	Became a jet pilot
1981	NASA chose Sally for the 7th Challenger shuttle flight
1982	Married Steve Hawley
1983	Became the first American woman to travel in space

1. Where _was Sally born_____ ? She was born in California.

2. When _____ ? She graduated from high school in 1969.

3. How many _____ ? She received two bachelor's degrees.

4. Where _____ ? She got her bachelors' degrees at Stanford University.

5. When _____ ? She got her Ph.D. in 1976.

6. What _____ ? Her major was physics.

7. Did _____ ? Yes, she did.

8. How long ago _____ ? She became a jet pilot ____ years ago.

9. What _____ ? NASA is the National Aeronautics and Space Agency.

10. Who _____ ? She married Steve Hawley.

11. When _____ ? In 1983.

B. The first woman astronaut to travel in outer space was not an American. Her name is Valentina Tereshkova. **In your encyclopedia, find out where she is from and when she first went into space. Write a short composition based on your research.**

Skill Objectives: Reading a chart; asking questions. Allow time for students to read the charted information about Sally Ride. Write questions words, *When? Where? What?* on the board. *Part A:* Have a volunteer ask his/her classmates questions about Sally Ride. The student answering may ask the next question. Encourage students to vary the form of the questions. After sufficient oral practice, call attention to the exercise. Complete one or more questions as a group, then assign the page for written work. *Part B:* Help students find information about Valentina Tereshkova or ask the school librarian to help them.

An Unlucky Day

The past progressive describes a continuing activity in the past. It is often used to describe something that was happening at the same time that something else happened. Look at the box for examples of the past progressive.

The phone rang when ⟨ I / he / it ⟩ was working.   The mail came when ⟨ you / we / they ⟩ were eating lunch.

ALSO: When I was working the phone rang; I was working when the phone rang.
When we were eating lunch the mail came; We were eating lunch when the mail came.

Yesterday was an unlucky day for George and his friends. Write what happened to everyone. The first one is done for you.

1. George

(cut) face; (shave)

He cut his face when he was shaving.

2. Sue

(hurt) arm; (play) tennis

_____
_____
_____

3. Barbara and Carla

dog (chase); (run)

_____
_____
_____

4. Tom

(find) fly; (eat) soup

_____
_____
_____

5. Jill and Art

(hit) tree; (drive)

_____
_____
_____

6. Pat

(burn) finger; (cook)

_____
_____
_____

DATA BANK

burn — burned	chase — chased	cut — cut
find — found	hit — hit	hurt — hurt

Skill Objective: Using the simple past and past progressive tenses. Teach/review the formation of the past progressive tense. Call attention to the example box at the top of the page. Have students note the relation between the two past actions: "The phone rang when he was working." The past progressive is an action going on, continuing, when the other (the past) takes place. Do the six items orally: "What happened to _____ when _____ was/were _____ing?" After sufficient oral practice, have students complete the page in writing.

Tina's Terrible Trip

Last winter Tina went to Miami for her vacation. She had a terrible time. Look at the picture story below.

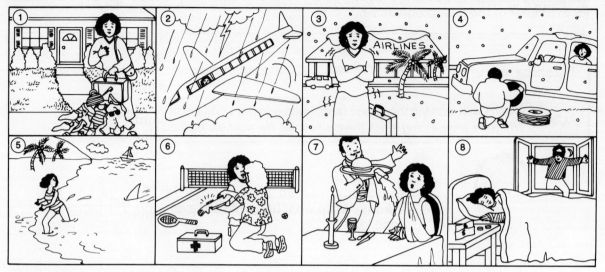

Write sentences about Tina's trip. The first one is done for you. Use it as a model for the others.

1. (leave) house; suitcase (open); clothes (fall) out *When she was leaving her house, her suitcase opened and her clothes fell out.*

2. (fly) to Miami; storm (begin) _____

   _____

3. (wait) for taxi; (snow) _____

   _____

4. (ride) to hotel; taxi (have) flat tire _____

   _____

5. (swim); shark (follow) her _____

   _____

6. (play) tennis; (break) arm _____

   _____

7. (eat) in restaurant; waiter (spill) water on her _____

   _____

8. (sleep); robber (break) into room and (steal) money _____

   _____

DATA BANK

begin — began	break —broke	fall — fell	have — had	steal — stole

Skill Objective: Using the simple past and past progressive tenses. Teach/review the verbs used on the page. Pantomime the first picture to illustrate the idea of two past actions occurring at the same time, one an ongoing activity (past progressive) and the other a sudden occurrence. Draw attention to the signal word "when." Do all eight sentences/pictures orally first. Encourage students to ask each other questions: "What happened to Tina when she was . . .?"

Susan B. Anthony: Fighting for People's Rights

A. Read Susan B. Anthony's story. Then circle the best answer for each question.

Susan B. Anthony was born in Massachusetts in 1820 and died in Rochester, N.Y., in 1906. In the 1850s, she saw many problems in her country and wanted to do something about them.

One of these problems was slavery. In those days, many states permitted people to own slaves. Susan B. Anthony thought all men and women should be free, so she fought against slavery. Slavery ended in 1865 after the U.S. Civil War, but there were other problems to solve.

Women did not have the right to vote in the United States in the early 1800s. Susan B. Anthony and many others felt that women and men should have equal rights. In 1869 she helped start the National Woman Suffrage Association. This group worked hard to get women the right to vote in the United States.

In 1869, Wyoming gave women the right to vote. Some other states also allowed women to vote. But Susan B. Anthony and the National American Woman Suffrage Association wanted all women to have the right to vote. They worked to amend, or add to, the Constitution of the United States. Finally, in 1920, fourteen years after Susan B. Anthony's death, the 19th Amendment was added to the Constitution. It gave all American women the right to vote.

1. What did Susan B. Anthony think about her country?
   a. It had no problems.
   b. It had many problems.
   c. It was fair to slaves.
   d. It was fair to women.

2. What did Susan B. Anthony do about slavery?
   a. She permitted people to own slaves.
   b. She fought against slavery.
   c. She started the Civil War.
   d. She voted against it.

3. What does "suffrage" mean?
   a. The right to vote.
   b. Slavery.
   c. Pain and discomfort.
   d. The right to fight.

4. Which of the following is true?
   a. In 1870 no American woman could vote in an election.
   b. In 1869 states gave women the right to vote in some elections.
   c. Susan B. Anthony had the right to vote in all elections.
   d. Some states gave women the right to vote before 1920.

5. How did women finally get the right to vote in the United States?
   a. The Civil War gave them the right to vote.
   b. An addition to the Constitution gave them the right to vote.
   c. Susan B. Anthony gave women the right to vote.
   d. Women got the right to vote when they went to work.

B. Elizabeth Cady Stanton was another woman who fought for women's rights in the United States. **Look in an encyclopedia to find out more about her and write on your own paper a short composition about her life.**

Skill Objectives: Reading a biography; making inferences; learning test-taking skills. Read the story aloud (or have students read it silently if you want this page to be "a test.") Go over new vocabulary such as *slavery, equal rights,* and *amend. Part A:* Do the first question together before assigning Part A as independent work. *Part B:* Students will need an encyclopedia for this. Help them to use it if necessary or encourage them to ask the school librarian for help.

Feelings

Use descriptions of situations to make inferences about feelings.

Here are some words that describe how people feel. Make sure you know what each word means.

angry	jealous	nervous	frightened	embarrassed
surprised	disappointed	bored	proud	sad

A. Read the paragraphs on this page and the next page. Decide what the person is probably feeling, and write the word in the blank. Be ready to explain your answers.

1. Tommy's parents were out for the evening. He was alone in the house. The telephone rang. No one was there when Tommy answered it. He thought he heard a noise downstairs. Outside, there was a storm. Tommy heard loud thunder and saw bright, flashing lightning. He locked the door of his room and tried to stay very quiet.

1. Tommy was feeling

   _____

2. Lorenzo's dog was missing. Every night after dinner Lorenzo went outside to look for his dog. He walked through the neighborhood and called, "Leal, Leal." One evening a police officer came to Lorenzo's house. He had Leal's collar, with Lorenzo's name and address on it. "I'm afraid your dog is dead," he told Lorenzo. "He was hit by a car." Lorenzo took the collar. He looked away from the police officer. He didn't say anything.

2. Lorenzo was feeling

   _____

3. The Phillips High School was having an art contest. Lisa walked into the room where her paintings were. There was a blue ribbon on one of her pictures. She was the grand prize winner. The judges gave her a check for $50.00. Lisa's friends and family congratulated her.

3. Lisa was feeling

   _____

4. Maria lives alone in New York City. Her parents live far away in San Juan, Puerto Rico. Maria didn't know it, but her parents were saving money so that they could come to visit her in New York. One night she heard a knock on the door. She looked through the peephole in the door and saw her parents standing in the hall.

4. Maria was feeling

   _____

5. Mr. Johnson was at the supermarket. He was in line, and the cashier was ringing up his groceries. She said "$41.82, please." Mr. Johnson reached into his pocket. He didn't have any money with him. He didn't have a check, either. Mr. Johnson couldn't pay for his groceries. His face turned red as he tried to explain the situation to the cashier.

5. He was feeling

   _____

(Go on to the next page.)

Skill Objectives: Interpreting characters' feelings; building vocabulary. Teach/review emotion vocabulary or have students find the words in dictionaries. Ask a volunteer to choose an emotion to pantomime. The class will try to guess the emotion. "Are you (bored)?" When the volunteer answers, "Yes, I am," ask, "Why are you (bored)?" Encourage the volunteer and members of the class to suggest reasons. If interest holds, cover all ten emotions in this manner. Read and complete the first item(s) on this page as a group, then assign pages 80 and 81 as independent work.

6. Jane's boyfriend Ray told the same stories all the time. All he ever talked about was his baseball team. She heard the same stories over and over again. Yesterday Ray was telling about the time he hit a home run in the ninth inning. Jane heard the story five or six times that week.

6. Jane was feeling

_____

7. Michel woke up early. Today was his big day. He thought he was going to become the new supervisor. He put on his best suit. He arrived at work early. He waited all day for the news. Finally at 5:00, the boss came into his office. He said, "Michel, I want you to meet Mr. Dubois, the new supervisor."

7. Michel was feeling

_____

8. Ms. Chin asked the neighborhood boys not to play ball near her house. They never obeyed. Whenever she heard the ball hit the side of the house, she yelled at the boys and told them to go away. Yesterday the boys hit a ball through her window. There was broken glass everywhere. Ms. Chin said that she was going to call the police.

8. Ms. Chin was feeling

_____

9. Mr. Smith was at the doctor's office. The doctor was in her laboratory. She was looking at Mr. Smith's X-rays. Mr. Smith was sitting, waiting for the doctor to come out. All the time he was wondering, "Am I sick or am I all right?" He was biting his fingernails the whole time.

9. Mr. Smith was feeling

_____

10. There was a school dance at the gymnasium. Rita walked into the gym and saw her old boyfriend, Sammy. He was dancing with his new girfriend, Pamela. They were laughing and having a good time. Rita watched them all evening long.

10. She was feeling

_____

B. Now write a paragraph about a time when you (or a friend or a made-up person) had one of these feelings. Use more paper if you need to.

_____

_____

_____

_____

_____

_____

_____

_____

Skill Objectives: Interpreting characters' feelings; building vocabulary. See annotation on page 80. *Part B:* Encourage students to title their paragraph with the feeling they choose to describe: "Jealous" or "Feeling Proud." Remind students that they do not have to describe something that really happened, they can make up a situation either realistic or fantastic. Have volunteers read their paragraphs aloud, without the title. The class can then guess how the character is feeling.

Dear Dot

Dear Dot—

My girlfriend Suzy and I were at the drive-in movies last night. We were both tired because we were working all day, but we wanted to go out for a little while to relax. The movie we were watching wasn't very interesting, but Suzy wanted to see the end of it anyway.

You aren't going to believe what happened next. We fell asleep. It was 2:30 when we woke up! Now Suzy's parents and my parents are angry. They don't want us to see each other any more. What can we do?

Danny

1. Where were Danny and Suzy last night? _____

2. Why were they tired? _____

3. Why did they go out? _____

4. What happened to Danny and Suzy last night? _____

_____

5. What time was it when they woke up? _____

6. Who is angry at Danny and Suzy? _____

_____

7. What does the word *relax* in this story mean? Circle the best answer.

    a. retire   b. sleep   c. spend   d. rest

8. What do you think Danny should do? Write your answer.

Dear Danny _____ ,

_____

_____

_____

_____

_____

_____

_____

_____

_____

Skill Objectives: Reading comprehension; understanding words through context; making judgments; writing a letter. Teach/ review the phrase "drive-in movie." Have students read the letter independently and answer questions 1-7. Correct these questions as a class. Encourage lively discussion of students' advice to Danny before having them write their Dear Dot letters to him. Extension Activity: a popular song from the 1950s or 60s, "Wake Up, Little Suzy" by the Everly Brothers retells this same predicament. If you can find this recording, your students should enjoy it.

Armando's Week

Look at Armando's school schedule. Then use it to finish the sentences. The first one is done for you.

Name of Student ___Armando Rodriguez___ Grade __8__ Homeroom __133__

	Day 1	Day 2	Day 3	Day 4	Day 5
Homeroom 7:30–7:40	→				
7:44–8:29	U.S. History	U.S. History	U.S. History	U.S. History	U.S. History
8:33–9:18	English	English	English	English	English
9:22–10:07	Typing	Typing	Study Period	Study Period	Typing
10:11–10:56	Science	Science	Science	Science	Science
11:00–11:25 / 11:28–11:53	Math	Math	Math	Math	Math
11:56–12:21	Lunch	Lunch	Lunch	Lunch	Lunch
12:25–1:10	Physical Education	Study Period	Physical Education	Physical Education	Study Period
1:14–2:00	French	French	French	French	French

1. Armando is in the ___8th___ grade.

2. His homeroom number is room _____.

3. Armando is in his homeroom every day from _____ to _____.
   (time)

4. Armando is in his U.S. History class _____ days a week.

5. He is in typing class _____ days a week.

6. His English class is from _____ to _____ every day.

7. He is in Physical Education _____ days a week.

8. His lunch time is _____ minutes.

9. His math class is _____ lunch.
   before—after

10. His science class is _____ his typing class.
    before—after

11. His _____ class is the last class of the day.

Skill Objective: Interpreting a school schedule. Have students examine the schedule. Ask questions such as the following: "Whose schedule is this? When is Armando in (homeroom)? At what time does he go to (English) class? How many days a week does Armando have (typing) class? When does Armando have (Study Period)? How long is a class period in Armando's school? How much time do students have between classes?" Encourage students to ask each other questions about the schedule. Assign the page for independent work. Correct as a class.

83

Helen Keller

A. Before you read the story, look at the Vocabulary Preview. Be sure that you know the meaning of each word. Use the dictionary. Some words have more than one meaning. The way the word is used in the story will help you decide the meaning you want. Write down the meanings of the words you are not sure of.

Vocabulary Preview

strength	communicate
blind	manual
deaf	celebrate
silent	eventually
immediately	hero

B. Now read the story. Use the dictionary if there are other words that you are not sure about. Notice that the words from the Vocabulary Preview are underlined.

Helen Keller and Anne Sullivan

The story of Helen Keller is a story of love, strength, and heroism. Helen Keller became blind and deaf when she was a baby. For six years she lived in a silent, lonely world. Her family loved her and tried to help her but they didn't know how. They wrote to the Perkins School for the Blind in Boston, Massachusetts. They asked the school to send a teacher for Helen.

Anne Sullivan took the train from Massachusetts to Alabama and met the Kellers. She began to work with Helen immediately. Anne Sullivan knew how to communicate with blind and deaf children. She took Helen's hand into her own and spelled words using the manual alphabet of the deaf.

Helen learned the letters quickly but she didn't understand that the letters were words and that the words had meanings. She thought that the moving fingers were a game that she and Anne Sullivan played for fun. Time went on. For days, weeks, and months, Anne Sullivan spelled thousands of words into the hand of her little student. Still, Helen did not understand.

April 5 was the big day. Helen was at the pump getting some water and Anne Sullivan spelled the word W-A-T-E-R into the child's hand. Helen spelled the word W-A-T-E-R back to Anne Sullivan. Helen began to touch other things. She wanted to know their names. Helen understood. Anne Sullivan called the family. She told them that Helen was finally able to communicate. After Helen learned the words "mother" and "baby," she touched Anne Sullivan. "What's your name?" she was asking. Anne spelled T-E-A-C-H-E-R. Everyone went into the house to celebrate this important day.

(Go on to the next page.)

Skill Objectives: Reading a biography; building vocabulary; understanding regular and irregular past tense. Allow time for students to look up vocabulary words in the dictionary and choose the appropriate definition. Review the definitions together. If you wish, read the selection aloud before asking students to read it silently.

Helen had much to learn. Anne Sullivan helped her to learn about the world. Eventually, Helen went to Radcliffe College and graduated with honors. After Helen learned to speak English she learned five other languages. Anne Sullivan was always with Helen to help her through her hard work.

Helen Keller told her story to people all over the world. She wanted others to know about the problems of the handicapped. Because of Helen Keller, many people began to understand the special needs of the handicapped. Helen Keller was a great woman and a hero to millions of people all over the world.

C. Use a word from the Vocabulary Preview to complete each of these sentences.

1. Juan graduated from high school with honors; he is going to _____ tonight.

2. The students were _____ while they were taking the tests.

3. When the radio broke, the pilot wasn't able to _____ with the tower.

4. That woman can't see at all; she's _____.

5. Mr. Jones rescued three children from a burning building; he's a _____.

D. Read these sentences. If the sentence is true, circle T. If it is false, circle F.

1. Helen became blind and deaf when she was six years old.	T F
2. Helen's family didn't know how to help her.	T F
3. The Perkins School was in Alabama.	T F
4. The Kellers lived in Massachusetts.	T F
5. Anne Sullivan traveled by plane to meet Helen.	T F
6. Anne Sullivan began to work with Helen right away.	T F
7. Anne Sullivan talked to Helen with her hands.	T F
8. Helen did not know that Miss Sullivan was "talking to her."	T F
9. Helen thought that she and Miss Sullivan were playing a game.	T F
10. Anne Sullivan spelled about two hundred words into Helen's hand.	T F
11. The first word that Helen understood was "water."	T F
12. The Keller family had a big party on April 5.	T F
13. Helen went to Radcliffe College.	T F
14. When she was older, Helen learned to speak.	T F
15. Everyone admired Helen Keller.	T F

Skill Objectives: Reading a biography; building vocabulary; understanding regular and irregular past tense. Students should complete the exercises on this page independently. Extension Activities: 1) Students can locate additional information about Helen Keller in their library. 2) Many sighted deaf people use American Sign Language. Your local library should have some good books about this language. Interested students can learn some of these signs and teach their classmates some new vocabulary in sign language and in English.

Combining Sentences

Look at the two sentences below:

   a. Tom is a student.
   b. Mary is a student.

These two sentences can be combined to make one sentence:

   Tom and Mary are students.

Combine the sets of sentences below to make one sentence from each set.

1. a. Kamala is from India.
   b. Krishnan is from India.

   1. _____

2. a. Kamala is from the northern city of New Delhi.
   b. Krishnan is from the western city of Bombay.

   2. _____

   _____

3. a. Kamala speaks Hindi.
   b. Krishnan speaks Konkani.

   3. _____

   _____

4. a. There are 179 different languages in India.
   b. Many people in India have to use English in order to communicate with each other.

   4. _____

   _____

5. a. Kamala speaks English.
   b. Krishnan speaks English.

   5. _____

6. a. Kamala met Krishnan at a university in Bombay.
   b. They got married two years later.

   6. _____

   _____

7. a. Kamala doesn't speak Konkani.
   b. Krishnan doesn't speak Hindi.   (NOTE: Use "so" after 7b.)
   c. They use English as their common language.

   7. _____

   _____

Now read all seven of the sentences you have written to tell the story of Kamala and Krishnan.

Skill Objective: Combining sentences with *and, but,* and *so.* Use information about your students to illustrate ways of combining sentences with *and, but,* and *so.* Examples: 1. *(Luis) is from Chile.* 2. *(Ana) is from Chile.* 3. *(Jean) is from Haiti.* 4. *(Carlos) lives five miles from school.* 5. *He takes the bus to school.* 6. *(Tai) lives two blocks from here.* 7. *She walks to school.* Help students combine different sentences with the appropriate conjunctions. Do the page as a group exercise before assigning as written work. The last part may also be a written activity.

In the Library

A. Ana Poleo wants a library card. Read the dialogue with a friend. One of you can be Ana. The other can be the librarian.

—Excuse me, I want to get a library card.

—Do you live here in town?

—Yes, I do.

—Good. Now you will need to have some proof of where you live. A letter addressed to you will do. Or perhaps you have a school ID card. You can also get a letter from a teacher.

—Does the card cost anything?

—No, it doesn't. But if you lose it, it costs 25¢ for a new one.

—Thank you. I'll bring my ID card tomorrow.

> No. **7381**
> MUNICIPAL PUBLIC LIBRARY
> extends borrowing privileges to
>
> Ana Poleo
>
> 23 Elm Street
>
> Smithfield
>
> Telephone 555-1234

B. Ana's library has all kinds of things in it. Look at the pictures. Use the Data Bank to write the name of each of the different things she can find there.

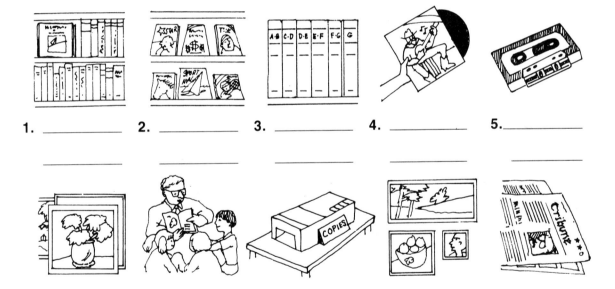

1. _____

2. _____

3. _____

4. _____

5. _____

6. _____

7. _____

8. _____

9. _____

10. _____

DATA BANK

copy machines	art exhibitions	tapes	pictures to rent	records	magazines
encyclopedias		books		newspapers	children's programs

Skill Objectives: Building vocabulary; learning about library resources. Teach/review new vocabulary in the dialogue. Allow students to practice the dialogue in pairs, then let two volunteers perform for the class. Discuss the information given on the library card. If possible, compare a local library card with the one shown on this page. *Part B:* Teach/review the vocabulary. As a class, identify and discuss the picture associated with each term. Assign the page for independent work.

Don Roberts, Delivery Man

Use picture clues to tell a story.
Then write the story.

A. Oral practice. Look at the pictures, and answer the questions that correspond to each picture. Work with a partner asking and answering the questions.

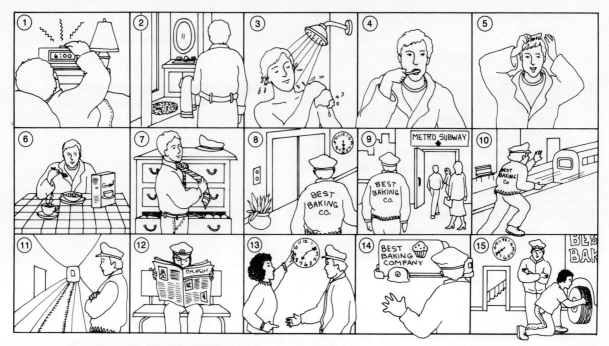

1. When did Don's alarm clock ring yesterday?
2. Where did he go after he got up?
3. What did he do there first?
4. and 5. After that, what did he do?
6. What did he have for breakfast?
7. What did he do after breakfast?
8. When did he leave his apartment?
9. Did he walk or take the bus to the subway?
10. Why was Don running fast?
11. Why was Don upset?
12. While he was waiting for the next train, what did he do?
13. Why did his boss shout at him?
14. When Don went to his truck, what did he see?
15. Did Don have a good day yesterday?

B. On your paper, write the story in paragraph form. Begin with a topic sentence.
Example: "Don Roberts had an interesting day yesterday."

C. Work with a partner or small group. Study the pictures above for one minute. Close your book and try to recall as many pictures as possible. Let each person in the group have one or more turns as you try to recall all fifteen pictures.

Skill Objectives: Reviewing past tense; telling a story from picture cues; writing a paragraph. *Part A:* This is an oral exercise. Have students examine the picture story. Introduce the character as Don Roberts. Have individual students contribute sentences to tell what happened in each frame. The story should be told in the past tense. When needed, ask questions about the pictures to guide the storyline and structure the verb tense. When all questions have been answered, have a volunteer tell the story to the class (or a partner) in his/her own words, using the questions/pictures as a guide. *Part B:* When students have had sufficient oral practice, ask them to write the story.

Choose the Verb Form

Present Progressive	Future (going to)	Past Progressive
Simple Present		Simple Past

Use the correct form of the verb in each sentence. Look at the five examples. There is one for each of the five tenses in the box. Use them as a model for your answers.

Examples: (write) 1. Bob ___is writing___ a letter now.
(write) 2. Bob ___writes___ a letter to his family every day.
(write) 3. Bob ___wrote___ to his father yesterday.
(write) 4. Bob ___was writing___ to his family when the phone rang.
(write) 5. Bob ___is going to write___ to his family next week.

(play) 1. Every Friday night my brothers _____ cards.

(take) 2. I _____ the bus to school every day.

(do) 3. Susan _____ her homework now.

(take) 4. My class _____ a field trip next week.

(watch) 5. Yesterday Ronald _____ TV for five hours.

(ride) 6. Tomorrow I _____ my bicycle to school.

(drive) 7. At the moment, Mr. and Mrs. Jones _____ to Miami.

(snow) 8. It _____ when I arrived in Chicago.

(have) 9. Marisa _____ a math class at 1:15 every Tuesday.

(read) 10. Mr. Chin _____ a chemistry book when the lights went off.

(see) 11. Last night I _____ a good movie.

(go) 12. Nick _____ to college after he graduates from high school.

(find) 13. Mr. Rodriguez _____ ten dollars in the street yesterday.

(die) 14. Maria's dog _____ three days ago.

(play) 15. Rosita _____ tennis when it started to rain.

(take) 16. Next month Kim _____ a vacation in Tokyo.

(speak) 17. My sister and I _____ five languages.

(sleep) 18. Be quiet! The baby _____.

(cut) 19. Pat _____ her finger while she was slicing tomatoes.

(buy) 20. Henry and John _____ a new car every three years.

Skill Objective: Comparing uses of verb tenses: simple present and past, present and past progressive, and future (going to).
Review the directions and examples with the students. Point out the spelling change in the example *write* (the silent *e* is dropped before adding *-ing*).
For added oral practice, have a student pantomime running, singing, drawing, etc. and have students ask and answer questions about the action in all five verb tenses. Students can check the spelling of past tense verbs by referring to the lists on pages 73 and 77.

89

Helping You Study: Alphabetical Order (4)

Many book titles begin with the word "A," "An," or "The." When you put book titles in alphabetical order, you do not include these words. Instead, you alphabetize by the second word, and follow the regular rules of alphabetical order. If two titles have the same second word, alphabetize by the third word, and so on.

A. Rewrite the following book titles in alphabetical order. The first one is done for you.

Title	Titles in Alphabetical Order
The Wind in the Willows	1. *The Adventures of Tom Sawyer*
A Tree Grows in Brooklyn	2. _____
The Call of the Wild	3. _____
An American Tragedy	4. _____
The Little Prince	5. _____
The Three Musketeers	6. _____
An Impossible Woman	7. _____
A Holiday for Murder	8. _____
A Farewell to Arms	9. _____
The Adventures of Tom Sawyer	10. _____

B. Check your work with your teacher or with another student. When you are sure you are correct, rewrite the following titles in alphabetical order

Title	Titles in Alphabetical Order
A Tale of Two Cities	1. _____
The Hat on the Bed	2. _____
The Sun Also Rises	3. _____
A Walk in the Dark	4. _____
An Old Friend from High School	5. _____
The Ice Age	6. _____
A Certain Slant of Light	7. _____
The Old Man and the Sea	8. _____
A Pocketful of Miracles	9. _____

Skill Objective: Alphabetizing book titles. Read the explanatory paragraph aloud. If you wish, have a student write the alphabet on the board for reference. Do several items in Part A with the class, then allow students to complete the exercise independently. Correct Part A together. Before assigning Part B, you may wish to write the following titles on the board for the class to alphabetize and discuss: *A Tale of Two Cities, Tale of Genji,* and *A Tangled Tale.* Let students complete Part B independently, then correct as a class.

Jesse James, a Famous Outlaw

Jesse James is one of the most famous outlaws, or criminals, in United States history. He robbed banks and trains from the late 1860s to the early 1880s.

Jesse James and his brothers fought for the South in the American Civil War. When the South lost the war, they were angry at the North. They started robbing Northern banks and railroads to show their hate for the North.

Most people were afraid of Jesse James. They thought he was a violent and dangerous man. Other people thought he was a hero. For more than ten years he and his gang robbed banks and trains, and they always got away.

In the 1870s, some members of Jesse's gang finally got caught. Only he and his brother Frank escaped. Jesse and Frank decided to hide. After three years, however, they started to rob banks again.

The government offered a large reward to the person who killed Jesse James. Robert Ford, a new member of Jesse James' gang wanted the reward. He killed Jesse James in 1882. Sheriffs and policemen all over the country were happy that the violence of Jesse James and his gang was over.

A TRAIN ROBBERY

A. Read the story about Jesse James. Then label each of the following sentences *Fact* or *Opinion*. The first two are done for you.

1. Jesse James robbed banks and trains. _Fact_

2. Jesse James was a hero. _Opinion_

3. Jesse James fought for the South in the Civil War. _____

4. United States criminals are the most violent in the world. _____

5. Jesse James was right to rob from the North. _____

6. Jesse James and his gang robbed banks and trains for many years. _____

7. The James brothers were cowards. _____

8. The James brothers hid from the police for three years. _____

9. Robert Ford killed Jesse James in 1882. _____

10. Robert Ford was wrong to kill Jesse James. _____

B. Outlaws are persons who consider themselves outside the law and feel free to break the law. Often they are considered heroes by people who share their beliefs or grievances. Robin Hood is a legendary English outlaw of 800 years ago. **Look in an encyclopedia to find out more about Robin Hood, and write a short composition about him. Why is he called "legendary"?**

Skill Objectives: Reading a biography; building vocabulary; distinguishing between fact and opinion. Before reading the story (aloud or silently) introduce the concept of an outlaw. Students will want to talk about some "bad guys" they know from literature, television, the movies, or their own experiences. Go over new vocabulary such as *hero, gang, cowards,* etc. *Part A:* Before assigning the page for independent work, do the first two items orally to be sure students remember the difference between fact and opinion. If they are having problems, do all ten sentences together. *Part B:* Encourage use of the encyclopedia to learn about Robin Hood.

Dear Dot

Dear Dot—

I am a Pisces. I was born on February 24. My girlfriend is a Capricorn. She was born in December. According to a book I have about horoscopes, Pisces and Capricorn are not a good combination. Pisces is a romantic and an artist. Capricorn is serious and businesslike. We get along well now, but what about the future? Do you think that I have to break up with my girlfriend?

Pisces

1. When was Pisces born? _____

2. When was his girlfriend born? _____

3. What does the book say about Pisces? _____

_____

4. What does the book say about Capricorn? _____

_____

5. What does the word *romantic* mean in his letter? Circle the best answer.

    a. dreamer   b. realistic   c. date   d. artistic

6. Write Dot's answer to Pisces. Tell him what he should do and should not do.

    Dear Pisces _____ ,

    _____

    _____

    _____

    _____

    _____

    _____

    _____

    _____

Commands

Imperatives are everywhere. Someone is always telling someone else what to do or what not to do. **Read the commands below. Where are you if you hear someone say the following?** The first answer is done for you.

1. "Pull in your stomach. Push out your chest. Keep your shoulders high. March, two, three, four. March, two, three, four."

   in the army

2. "Pay attention. Listen quietly. Don't talk and don't copy anyone else's paper."

   _____

3. "Take two of these every three hours. Drink a lot of liquids. Come back and see me in three days if you don't feel better."

   _____

4. "Don't get too close to the animals. Don't give them any food and don't tease them, please." _____

5. "Empty the trash. Wash the dishes. Play with your little brother. Be quiet."

   _____

6. "Fasten your seat belts. Don't smoke. Stay in your seats until we are off the ground."

   _____

7. "Put on your signal. Slow down. Take the turn. Give it some more gas. Keep going."

   _____

8. "Jump up and down. Stretch your arms out. Touch your toes. Don't bend your knees."

   _____

9. "Walk downstage. Take a deep breath. Look at the audience. Say your lines."

   _____

10. "Bend your knees a little. Dig your poles into the ground. Give yourself a little push and you're off."_____

D A T A B A N K

in an airplane	in the army	in a car	in a classroom
at the doctor's office	at exercise class	at home	at the zoo
on a mountain	in a theater		

Skill Objectives: Recognizing imperatives; drawing conclusions. Read the introductory paragraph aloud. Explain the word *imperatives*. Read and solve the first one or two examples as a group, then assign the page for independent work.

93

Opposites

Look at each numbered word. Find the opposite word in the Data Bank, and write it on the line. Then put a check next to the word in the Data Bank. The first one is done for you.

1. beautiful   _ugly_

2. never   _____

3. married   _____

4. boring   _____

5. sick   _____

6. worst   _____

7. unfriendly   _____

8. cheap   _____

9. right   _____

10. back   _____

11. fast   _____

12. difficult   _____

13. answer   _____

14. whispering   _____

15. going   _____

16. stupid   _____

17. late   _____

18. selling   _____

19. forget   _____

20. last   _____

21. begin   _____

22. arrive   _____

23. withdraw   _____

24. bottom   _____

25. hated   _____

26. evening   _____

27. noisy   _____

28. loser   _____

29. shut   _____

30. drying   _____

31. safe   _____

32. heavy   _____

DATA BANK

always	end	leave	shouting
best	expensive	light	single
buying	first	loved	slow
coming	friendly	morning	top
dangerous	front	open	ugly ✔
deposit	healthy	question	washing
early	intelligent	quiet	winner
easy	interesting	remember	wrong

Skill Objectives: Recognizing opposites; learning test-taking skills. Read the directions aloud. Explain that checking off words in the Data Bank is a helpful test-taking technique. It reduces the number of answer choices for the next questions. Tell students to skip difficult items and complete the easy ones. Then they can return to the difficult items and choose the best answer from the few remaining choices. Do several items as a class, then assign the page for independent work.

94

How Does It Work?

Most Americans use clothes washers to clean their clothes, but many people don't know how a clothes washer really works. Here is a short explanation.

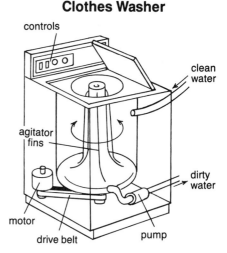

Clothes Washer

A clothes washer has many controls. You use the controls to turn the machine on, to select hot, cold, or warm water, and to set the time for the wash. When you turn the machine on, clean water comes in from the hot or cold water hoses. The water mixes with the detergent to clean the clothes in the drum. Water and detergent are not enough to clean the clothes. A motor in the clothes washer pulls the agitator fins of the drum back and forth. The movement, water, and detergent clean the clothes. When the clothes are clean, a pump pushes the dirty water out through the dirty water hose. The motor spins the drum of the clothes washer very fast. After the clothes spin for a few minutes, the clothes washer turns itself off, and the clothes are ready to go in a clothes dryer or on a clothes line to dry.

A. Read the article, look at the diagram and answer the following questions. Circle your answers.

1. According to the diagram, which of the following helps the motor turn the agitator fins?

   a. the clean water hoses   b. the drive belt   c. the pump

2. What happens while the clothes are spinning for the final few minutes?

   a. They get clean.

   b. The motor rips them.

   c. They become less wet.

3. Use the numbers 1 through 5 to show the sequence in which things happen when you wash your clothes in a clothes washer.

   _____ Hot, cold, or warm water comes into a machine.

   _____ The clothes washer turns itself off.

   _____ The motor pulls the agitator fins back and forth.

   _____ Turn on the machine at the controls.

   _____ The pump pushes out the dirty water.

B. Read about how a clothes dryer works. In your own words write an explanation of the process, and draw a diagram of the important parts of a clothes dryer.

Skill Objectives: Reading a technical article; interpreting a diagram; making inferences; sequencing. Have students read the article silently. Tell them to look at the diagram as each part is mentioned. They may want to reread one or more times to be sure they undertand how the washing machine works. *Part A:* Tell students that they are going to scan, or look quickly through the article, to find specific information that will help them answer the questions. *Part B:* Students can find information about clothes dryers in books or encyclopedias. The school librarian can help them locate this information.

95

I Disagree!

David and Diane are twins, but they never agree about anything. If one says a certain day was cold, the other says it was hot. They always disagree. **Look at David and Diane's statements below. Write what the other twin said on the line provided. Write your answer in a complete sentence.** The first two are done for you.

David

1. The boys were right.

2. *The glass was empty.*

3. We were noisy.

4. _____

5. The tickets were expensive.

6. _____

7. The room was clean.

8. _____

9. It was sunny.

10. _____

11. The stories were wonderful.

12. _____

13. The dogs were huge.

14. _____

15. The animals were wild.

16. _____

17. His hair was straight.

18. _____

19. The sandwiches were thick.

20. _____

Diane

1. *The boys were wrong.*

2. The glass was full.

3. _____

4. The store was open.

5. _____

6. He was guilty.

7. _____

8. The floor was wet.

9. _____

10. The bread was fresh.

11. _____

12. They were rich.

13. _____

14. The classes were interesting.

15. _____

16. The roads were dangerous.

17. _____

18. It was an odd number.

19. _____

20. The children were sick.

D A T A   B A N K

tame	curly	thin	quiet	dirty	empty	healthy	terrible
dry	tiny	safe	cheap	even	rainy	boring
wrong	poor	closed	stale	innocent

Skill Objectives: Recognizing opposites; building vocabulary. As a warm-up activity, put a few words on the board such as *hot-cold*, *black-white*, *tall-_____* , *happy-_____* . Have volunteers fill in the blanks. Provide more examples if you wish to. Then read the directions aloud. To be sure students understand, try the first few items together. Call attention to the Data Bank. Tell students to skip difficult items and complete the easy ones, checking them in the Data Bank. Then they can return to the difficult ones and use the Data Bank to figure out the few remaining choices. Assign the page for independent work.

Helping You Study:
Using the Card Catalog

Nearly every library has a card catalog. There are cards in the catalog for all the books in the library. You can look in the card catalog and find the title or author of any book that the library owns.

The cards in the catalog are in alphabetical order. Authors are listed by last name. Titles are listed by first word except for "a," "an," and "the."

The cards are in drawers. On the front of each drawer is a label. The label tells what cards are in the drawer.

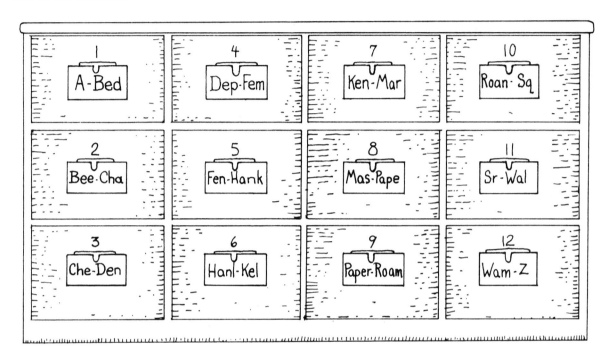

Look at the picture of the card catalog drawers above. In which drawer would you find each of the following authors and titles? The first one is done for you.

The Gallant Five	5	*The Adventures of Ulysses*	_____
E.B. White	_____	*Too Near the Sun*	_____
Rain or Shine	_____	*A Fabulous Creature*	_____
The World of Animals	_____	Shirley Jackson	_____
Ray Bradbury	_____	*How To Fix Cars*	_____
Conquistadors	_____	Agatha Christie	_____
Mark Twain	_____	*Bright Candles*	_____
Never Is a Long, Long Time	_____	Kurt Vonnegut	_____
Judy Blume	_____	Norma Klein	_____

Skill Objective: Locating card catalog entries. Read the explanatory paragraph aloud. Ask volunteers to name two authors and two book titles. Write these on the board. Help students decide in which card catalog drawer they would look to find each. Do one or two items together, then assign this page for independent work. Extension Activity: Discuss the types of books written by the authors listed here. Encourage students to choose an author to look up in the catalog of the library and read a short story or novel by that author.

Emergency!

A. **What do you do if someone you know accidentally swallows poison or pills? Read the list below and find out.**

FIRST AID—POISON

1. ***Stay calm.***
2. Look for the pill or poison container.
3. Call the emergency room of a hospital or the Poison Control Center.
4. Tell the health professional the name of the pill or poison and how much the victim swallowed.
5. Follow the directions of the health professional.
6. If they ask you to go to the hospital, bring the pill or poison container with you.
7. Do not give the victim any liquids unless the health professional tells you to.
8. Do not make the victim vomit unless the health professional tells you to.
9. Do not give any salt solution (salt mixed with any liquid).

B. **Use the information in the list to answer the following questions.**

1. What is the first thing to do in a poisoning emergency?

   _____

2. What do you do before you call the hospital or poison center?

   _____

3. What information are you going to give the health professional?

   _____

4. If you take the victim to the hospital, what are you going to bring with you?

   _____

5. What two things are you not going to do unless the doctor tells you to?

   _____

6. What is a salt solution? _____

7. What is a health professional? _____

Skill Objectives: Following directions; using imperatives; understanding words through context. Have students read the emergency instructions silently, then name any unknown words. Let other students explain the words, or define them yourself. Go over some or all of the questions as a class, then assign for written work. Extension Activity: At home, have students copy directions printed on food containers, appliances, etc. As students read these directions aloud, their classmates can guess where they were written.

Which One Is Correct?

Be careful with present tense verbs after *who* and *that.* Look at the following examples to help you to understand which form of the verb to use.

John is a boy who **likes** cake.

Singular: The computer is a tool that **makes** work easy.

This is the book that **tells** about fixing cars.

My friends are boys who **like** cake.

Plural: Computers are tools that **make** work easy.

These are the books that **tell** about fixing cars.

Now look at the following sentences. Choose the correct form of the verb according to the examples above and circle it. The first one is done for you.

1. Karen is a girl who (like, (likes)) to smile.

2. Those are the boys who (know, knows) the answer to the question.

3. José is an athlete who (run, runs) five miles every day.

4. New York is a city that (have, has) a lot of people.

5. Surgeons are doctors who (operate, operates) on people.

6. The Red Cross is an organization that (help, helps) people.

7. This is my cousin who (live, lives) in Baltimore.

8. Cats are animals that (sleep, sleeps) most of the day.

9. Mr. Davis is the man who (clean, cleans) our school.

10. This is the key that (lock, locks) the back door.

11. The mail carrier is the person who (deliver, delivers) the mail.

12. The secretaries are the ones who (open, opens) the mail.

13. A photographer is a person who (take, takes) pictures.

14. Reporters are people who (write, writes) the news.

15. Tomás is a man who (speak, speaks) eight different languages.

16. A globetrotter is a person who (travel, travels) all around the world.

17. There are some whales that (weigh, weighs) more than 60 tons.

18. Electronics is a subject that (interest, interests) many people.

19. Kangaroos are animals that (carry, carries) their babies in pouches.

20. Florida is a state that (export, exports) a lot of fruit.

21. The eucalyptus is a tree that (grow, grows) mainly in Australia.

22. Ecuador and Peru are the countries that (lie, lies) to the south of Colombia.

23. Stars are heavenly bodies that (have, has) their own light and heat.

24. A mechanic is a person who (fix, fixes) cars.

25. Artists are men and women who (paint, paints) pictures.

Skill Objectives: Reviewing simple present tense; using adjective clauses with *who* and *that*. Call attention to the examples at the top of the page. When the word that precedes *who* or *that* is singular, the verb that follows *who* or *that* is singular. When the word is plural, the verb is plural. Complete the first few sentences as an oral group activity. Then assign the page for independent written work.

99

Dear Dot

Dear Dot—

I couldn't understand any English last year. I studied hard, and now I can speak English pretty well. The problem is my family. Now that I can speak English, no one else in my family is learning it. They depend on me to translate all the time. At first I liked the practice and I liked to be so important. Now I am spending too much time doing my brothers' English homework and translating for the rest of my family at the doctor's office, the supermarket, and the bank. What can I do?

Translator

1. How did Translator learn to speak English? _____

_____

2. Why did Translator like to translate at first? _____

_____

3. How does Translator help her brothers? _____

4. Where does Translator help her family? _____

_____

5. What does the word *pretty* mean in this letter? Circle the best answer.

   a. beautiful   b. nice   c. fairly   d. not very

6. What is your advice to Translator? Write a letter telling her what you think she can do to solve her problem.

   Dear Translator _____ ,

   _____

   _____

   _____

   _____

   _____

   _____

   _____

   _____

Skill Objectives: Reading comprehension; understanding words through context; making judgments; writing a letter. Teach/review the phrase *depend on*. Have students read the letter independently and answer questions 1-5. Correct the answers as a class. Encourage discussion of what Dot's advice to Translator should be. Ask students if their families depend on them to translate. How do they feel about the situation? Finally, have them write letters to Translator giving her their advice.

100

The Fifty States

The United States of America has fifty separate states, united or joined together into one nation. Forty-eight of the states are in the land between Canada and Mexico. The other two states are Alaska and Hawaii. Alaska is far north of the other states, on the northwest border of Canada. Hawaii is a group of islands in the Pacific Ocean. Alaska and Hawaii are the newest states. They became states in 1959.

Alaska, Texas, California, and Montana are large states. California is the largest state in population, and Alaska is the largest state in area. New York, Texas, Pennsylvania, Illinois, and Ohio are also states with large populations. The smallest state in area is Rhode Island. The smallest state in population is also the largest state in area—Alaska! The capital of the United States is Washington, D.C. It is not in any state but in the District of Columbia.

A. Read the passage about the fifty states. Then label each of the following sentences *Fact* **or** *Opinion.* **The first one is done for you.**

1. Hawaii is one of the states in the United States. _Fact_____

2. Hawaii is the best place to live in the United States. _____

3. It is too cold to live in Alaska. _____

4. Two large states are Texas and California. _____

5. Alaska and Hawaii are the newest states. _____

6. The population of a state is more important than its size. _____

7. Alaska is the smallest state in population. _____

8. California has too large a population. _____

B. Read the passage again. Then look at the following sentences. Write *T* **if the sentence is true, write** *F* **if it is false, and write** *?* **if the passage does not give you enough information. The first two are done for you.**

___T___ 1. Alaska and Montana are large states.

___?___ 2. Florida is the fastest-growing state.

_____ 3. Alaska is the largest in area and population.

_____ 4. The District of Columbia is in the state of Washington.

_____ 5. It is always hot in Texas.

_____ 6. Rhode Island's population is only four million.

_____ 7. Hawaii is one of the newest states.

_____ 8. Most Californians are immigrants.

Skill Objectives: Reading for detail; distinguishing between fact and opinion; completing true/false/? statements. Teach/review any new or difficult vocabulary. Read the selection aloud and have students reread it silently. Tell them they can refer to it as often as they need to as they answer the questions. Do the first two examples in Parts A and B together before assigning the page for written work. Be sure students understand that the *?* answer in Part B is used for any statement for which the passage does not provide information. (For example, item 2 may in fact be true or it may in fact be false, but there is nothing about it in the passage, so it is marked *?*.)

101

A Map of the United States

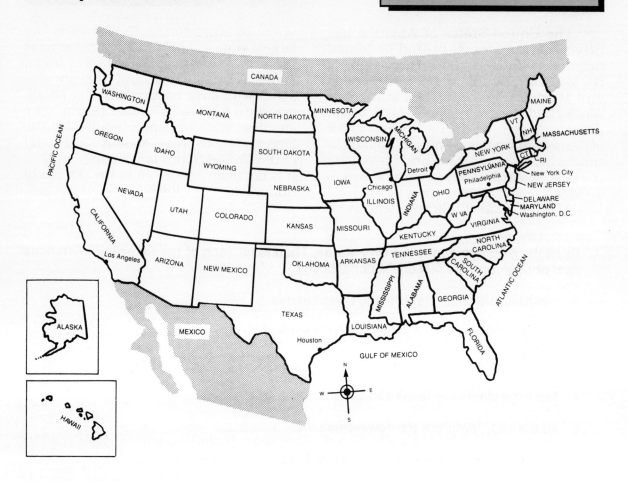

A. Use the map to answer these questions. Write short answers.

1. Name 5 northern states.

   _____ _____ _____ _____ _____

2. Name 5 southern states.

   _____ _____ _____ _____ _____

3. Name 5 eastern states.

   _____ _____ _____ _____ _____

4. Name 3 western states.

   _____ _____ _____

5. Name 5 northeastern states.

   _____ _____ _____ _____ _____

6. Name 8 states that begin with the letter *M*.

   _____ _____ _____ _____

   _____ _____ _____ _____

(Go on to the next page.)

Skill Objectives: Interpreting a political map; categorizing. Use the United States map as a basis for free discussion. Have students locate their state and list other states they have lived in or traveled through. Draw attention to the compass rose. Teach/review the map directions. Ask, "What state is (west) of (Texas)?" Encourage students to ask each other similar questions. Teach/review the terms Southeastern/Northeastern/ Southwestern/Northwestern United States. *Part A:* Let students complete the items on this page and the top of page 103 independently, then compare and discuss their answers.

102

7. Name a city in Texas.

_____

8. Name a city in California.

_____

9. Name a city in Michigan.

_____

10. Name a city in Pennsylvania.

_____

11. Name a city in Illinois.

_____

12. Name the United States Capital.

_____

B. Odd Man Out: Cross out the word that does not belong. Write the topic or category on the line above each group. The first one is done for you.

1. _states_
   Kansas
   Utah
   ~~Los Angeles~~
   Oklahoma

2. _____
   Missouri
   Chicago
   Houston
   Philadelphia

3. _____
   Gulf of Mexico
   Atlantic Ocean
   Pacific Ocean
   Canada

4. _____
   Alaska
   Hawaii
   Puerto Rico
   Virginia

5. _____
   States
   North
   South
   East

6. _____
   Country
   City
   State
   President

7. _____
   Colorado
   Ohio
   Connecticut
   California

8. _____
   Iowa
   Utah
   Maine
   Ohio

C. What state do you live in? What do you know about it? Find the following information about your state in an encyclopedia or almanac or by asking your teachers.

1. Where is it located? (southeast? northwest? etc.)
2. What is the total state population?
3. What is the state capital?
4. What is the largest city in population?
5. Are there any mountains, deserts, volcanoes? Do earthquakes happen often?
6. What crops, products, or industries is your state famous for?

Write a paragraph about your state which includes the information you learned. Use more paper if you need to.

I live in _____

_____

_____

_____

_____

_____

Skill Objectives: Interpreting a political map; categorizing; learning/writing about a state. *Part B:* Discuss the first example and elicit that Los Angeles is crossed out because it is not a state as the others are. Have students complete items 2 through 8 individually or in pairs; discuss and correct them as a class. (Spelling is a factor in #7 and 8.) *Part C:* Students can work individually or in small groups to find the information about their state. This could be an extended writing project which could include pictures or postcards. Students might choose to put their information into letter form instead of a simple paragraph.

103

The United States: A Geography Lesson

The United States is a large country with many different things to see and learn about.

There are long rivers and big lakes. The Mississippi River is a very big river in the central part of the country. It is 2,350 miles long, and it divides the country into the East and the West. The Great Lakes (Lake Superior, Lake Erie, Lake Huron, Lake Michigan and Lake Ontario) are in the north. These are very large fresh-water lakes. They are important for transportation and industry.

There are two major groups of mountains in the United States. The Appalachian Mountains are in the East. They are very old mountains and not very high. The Rocky Mountains are in the West. They are quite large. Some are 14,000 feet high.

The middle of the United States, between these two mountain ranges, is a 1,500 mile plain. A plain is a large flat area of land with few trees. Many of this country's large farms are on this plain. A trip across the United States is an interesting experience. It is a lot of fun and a good lesson in geography.

A. Read these sentences. If the sentence is true, circle T. If the sentence is false, circle F.

1. The Mississippi River is 2,350 miles long.   T   F

2. There are six Great Lakes.   T   F

3. The Great Lakes are salt-water lakes.   T   F

4. The Rocky Mountains are in the West.   T   F

5. A plain is a group of mountains.   T   F

B. What is this reading mostly about? Circle the best answer.

a. the Great Lakes

b. the Rocky Mountains

c. the United States

d. the Mississippi River

C. Read the paragraphs at the top of the page again. Then label the features shown on the map of the mid-continental United States below.

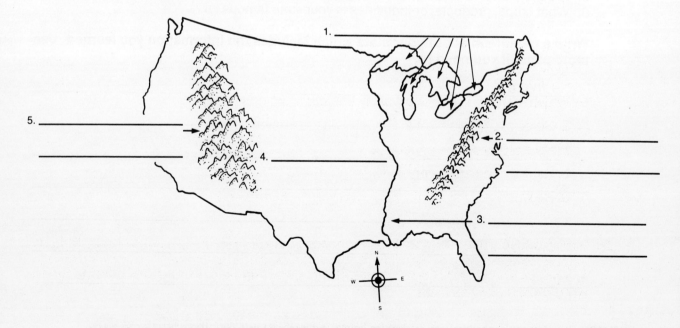

Skill Objectives: Identifying main idea and details; interpreting a topographic map. Read the selection aloud. Teach/discuss any new or difficult vocabulary. Have students reread the selection silently, then complete the three Parts independently. Correct and discuss their answers as a class.

Travels With Charley

John Steinbeck is one of America's greatest writers. Many of his novels and short stories are about people with troubles and problems. *Travels With Charley* is different; it's a book about traveling around the United States. John Steinbeck and Charley traveled together from New York to Maine and then to the Midwest. From the Midwest, they went west to California. On their way back East, they visited Texas. Finally, John and Charley traveled through the South, and back up north to New York.

John Steinbeck's journey took three months to complete. When he got home, he wrote about what he saw when he crossed the country. He decided that Americans were wonderful people, and that the U.S. was full of peaceful towns, great cities, and beautiful parks. Charley seemed to enjoy the trip, although he didn't say or write anything. You might wonder why Charley had no ideas about America. The reason is: he was John Steinbeck's dog, a big black-blue French poodle.

A. Answer the following questions. Circle your answers.

1. John Steinbeck started and ended his trip in

    a. California   b. Maine   c. the Midwest   d. New York

2. How is *Travels With Charley* different from John Steinbeck's other books?

    a. His other books are about cats, not dogs.

    b. His other books are about people who travel in Canada.

    c. His other books are about people with problems.

    d. His other books take place in foreign countries.

3. The reading says that John Steinbeck's journey took three months. A journey is

    a. a trip   b. a journal   c. a country   d. a novel

4. John Steinbeck most likely took Charley with him because

    a. he couldn't find anyone to take care of the dog.

    b. he wanted company, but not human company.

    c. he wanted to write a story about a traveling dog.

    d. he had no other friends to go with him.

5. Which of the following is probably true about John Steinbeck?

    a. He enjoyed his travels around the United States.

    b. He didn't like dogs or people.

    c. He crossed the country as fast as possible.

    d. He was a careful man who liked to stay close to home.

B. Use an encyclopedia to find out: where and when John Steinbeck was born, where he went to school, the names of his famous books, a brief summary of one of his books, any prizes and awards he won, and where and when he died. Use this information to write a short composition.

Skill Objectives: Reading for details; making inferences; learning test-taking skills. Tell students that this reading is about someone who traveled through the United States. Read the passage aloud, then have students reread it silently. Suggest that they follow the author's route on the map on page 102. You may want to show a copy of *Travels With Charley* to the students and let them browse through it after they have completed this page. *Part A:* Have students complete the five items independently or in pairs. Discuss the answers after they have finished. *Part B:* The school librarian can help students find information about Steinbeck.

Street Directions

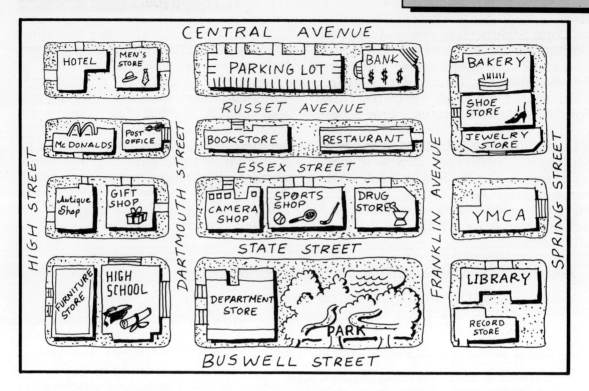

A. Read the directions. Trace the path on the map. Then answer the questions.

1. You are in the park. Walk up Franklin Avenue and take a left on to Essex Street. Walk into the store between the camera shop and the drug store.

   a. Where are you? _____

   b. What can you buy there? _____

2. You are in the bakery. Walk down Franklin Avenue and take a right on to State Street. Walk one block, then take a left on to Dartmouth Street. You are in the building across from the high school.

   a. Where are you? _____

   b. What can you buy there? _____

3. You are coming out of McDonald's. Walk down Essex Street until you come to Franklin Avenue, then take a right. Follow Franklin Avenue to the end, to Buswell Street. You are at the store at the corner of Buswell and Franklin.

   a. Where are you? _____

   b. What can you buy there? _____

4. You are in the furniture store. Walk two blocks up High Street and take a right onto Russet Avenue. Go to the end of Russet and enter the store next to the bakery.

   a. Where are you? _____

   b. What can you buy there? _____

(Go on to the next page.)

Skill Objectives: Reading a city map; following directions. *Part A:* Examine the map with the students. Discuss the stores and public buildings found in the area. Read and follow the first set of directions as a group. Let volunteers answer both questions. Assign the page as independent work. Extension Activity: Encourage interested students to draw a map of part of the downtown area of their town or city, labeling the streets and buildings.

B. Look at the map on the facing page. Read the problems below. Study the map, then write the street directions. The words in the Data Bank will help you. The first problem is done for you.

1. You are shopping at the department store and you want to go back to your hotel. How do you get from the department store to the hotel?

   Walk up Dartmouth Street to Russet Avenue. Take a left on

   Russet Avenue, and the hotel is next to the men's store.

2. Susan is staying at the hotel. She wants to visit the jewelry store. How can she get there?

   _____

   _____

   _____

3. How do you get from the library to the Post Office?

   _____

   _____

   _____

4. How do you get from the bakery to the high school?

   _____

   _____

   _____

5. You're at McDonald's and you want to go to the park. How do you get there?

   _____

   _____

   _____

D A T A   B A N K

at the corner	on the left/right	next to	take a left/right
walk down	walk up	walk two blocks	between

C. Answer these questions. Refer to the map if you need to. Use short answers. The first one is done for you.

1. Is the high school across from the bank?   *No, it isn't.*

2. Is the sports shop near the park?   _____

3. Does a bakery sell fruit?   _____

4. Can you buy film in a record store?   _____

5. Can you buy shoes at a library?   _____

Skill Objectives: Reading a city map; writing street directions. *Part B:* Teach/review the phrases in the Data Bank. Do the first item together as a class, having the students trace the route, step by step. Have them complete items 2–5 independently or in pairs. *Part C:* This gives students an opportunity to review spelling of abbreviations. If they have difficulty, discuss where the apostrophe belongs and point out that it stands for a letter or letters that have been omitted. As an extension activity for this page, have volunteers write directions to a mystery location on the map. Classmates must follow them.

107

Helping You Study:
What Kind of Book?

We can divide the books in the library into three basic groups: fiction, non-fiction, and biography. Read the definitions of these basic groups.

Fiction	Stories that come from an author's imagination. Novels, mysteries, love stories, and space adventures are all works of fiction.
Non-fiction	Factual books about science, geography, history, mathematics, art, and medicine are works of non-fiction.
Biography	The life story of a person, usually a famous person. An autobiography is a book in which one person, usually someone famous, tells his or her own life story.

Sometimes you can decide if a book is fiction, non-fiction or biography by looking at the title and author. **Look at the following list. Write the name of the group in which each book belongs.** The first one is done for you.

1. *George Washington* by James Flexner _____biography_____

2. *The Age of Electronics* by C.F.T. Overhage _____

3. *The Story of My Life* by Helen Keller _____

4. *100 Years of Baseball* by Lee Allen _____

5. *Mahatma Gandhi* by Vincent Sheehan _____

6. *The Mystery of the Blue Train* by Agatha Christie _____

7. *Mao Tse Tung* by Stephen Ulhalley _____

8. *The Champion's Guide to Bowling* by Dick Weber _____

9. *Mystery of the Haunted House* by Mary Bonner _____

10. *The Last Days of Martin Luther King* by Jim Bishop _____

11. *Journey Beyond Tomorrow* by Robert Sheckley _____

12. *Let's Get Well* by Adele Davis _____

13. *Space War Blues* by Richard Lupoff _____

14. *The Memoirs of Richard Nixon* by Richard Nixon _____

15. *Radio's Golden Age* by Frank Buxton _____

16. *Love and Mary Ann* by Catherine Cookson _____

Skill Objective: Understanding library classification. Allow time for students to read the introductory paragraphs silently. Explain any difficult or unfamiliar words. Classify several items as an oral group activity, then assign the page as independent work.

What Were They Doing?

Read each of the following stories. Tell what the people were doing.

1. Liem drove into the driveway. The back seat of his car was full of paper bags filled with food, soda, detergent and other household items.

   What was he doing? *He was shopping for groceries.* _____

2. It was a hot day. Marguerite put down her brush. Her hair and clothes had little spots of white on them. She went into the house to get a cool drink before continuing her work.

   What was she doing? _____

3. Billy's father came into his room. He told him, "It's late at night. Go to sleep." He took away Billy's flashlight and book.

   What was Billy doing? _____

4. Rudy and Donna were very happy as they came into the house. "Look at these four big ones we caught!" they said. "We can make a delicious supper out of them."

   What were they doing? _____

5. Roberto was greasy and dirty. He look tired, but he was happy. "I don't have to walk to work tomorrow," he said. "I finally got it to work."

   What was Roberto doing? _____

6. Sandra counted the words on the page. There were 250 words. Her teacher said, "That's very good work for five minutes. You are going to be a great secretary."

   What was Sandra doing? _____

7. Mrs. Anderson came into the house. Her hands were wet. She said to her husband, "Everything in the garden was dying of thirst. Linda didn't do any of her yard chores while we were on vacation."

   What was Mrs. Anderson doing? _____

8. René and Jules were soaking wet. They put away the pet shampoo and the special towel they used for Spot. "Well, he growled and barked a lot, but he's finally clean," said René.

   What were the boys doing? _____

9. Mr. Yu put away the dustpan and broom. He threw the glass into the waste basket. "I'm glad I got that broken bottle before any of the children stepped on it," he told his wife.

   What was Mr. Yu doing? _____

10. Mrs. Hernandez put down her red pencil. "That's the last one," she said to her husband. "Most of the students did very well. There were more than 8 students who got A's, and only 2 who got F's."

    What was Mrs. Hernandez doing? _____

Dear Dot

Dear Dot—

I have a question. I asked my sister Betty to let me wear her blue dress to the school dance. Betty's clothes are so pretty, and I wanted to look nice. That night at the dance, Bob Johnson spilled coffee on me. It was an accident. Unfortunately, the coffee stained the dress and ruined it. Betty says it is my fault. I say it is Bob's fault. Whose fault is it? Whose responsibility is it to buy Betty a new dress?

Innocent

1. Why did Innocent want to wear Betty's dress? _____

_____

2. What happened at the dance? _____

_____

3. What did the accident do to Betty's dress? _____

4. What does the word *innocent* at the end of this letter mean? Circle the best answer.

   a. not ready   b. not happy   c. not guilty   d. not free

5. Discuss Innocent's letter with your classmates and decide who is responsible. Then write a letter telling Innocent what you think she should do and should not do.

Dear Innocent _____ ,

   _____

_____

_____

_____

_____

_____

                                                    _____

Skill Objectives: Reading comprehension; understanding words through context; making judgments; writing a letter. Have students read the letter silently, then independently complete questions 1-4. Correct these as a class. Encourage lively discussion of the proper advice to give Innocent, then have students write their letters giving her their advice.

What's the Weather?

A. Look at the map and write today's weather for each city.

1. Miami. *It's hot and sunny in Miami. It's about 90°.*

2. Seattle. _____

3. Los Angeles. _____

4. Chicago. _____

5. Houston. _____

6. New York. _____

B. What's tomorrow's weather? **Look at the chart below and write a weather report for tomorrow in the same cities.**

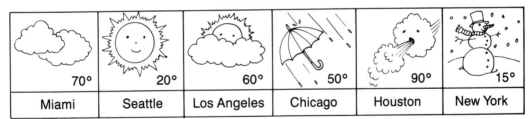

70°	20°	60°	50°	90°	15°
Miami	Seattle	Los Angeles	Chicago	Houston	New York

It's going to be cloudy and warm in Miami tomorrow, about 70°.

_____

_____

_____

_____

_____

_____

Skill Objectives: Reading a weather map; using Fahrenheit temperatures; reviewing weather vocabulary. *Part A:* Discuss the weather map and review the vocabulary. If your students are unaccustomed to thinking of temperature in Fahrenheit degrees, call attention to the Fahrenheit scale at the right and tell them that this is the usual way of talking about temperature in the United States. Review the vocabulary and assign for independent work. *Part B:* This asks students to use the "be going to" future form. Do a few examples before assigning Part B as written work. As an extension, students may wish to write an imaginary weather report for their area.

What's the Temperature?

Normal Average Temperatures (in Fahrenheit)

Place	Winter JAN.	Spring APR.	Summer JULY	Fall OCT.
Miami, Florida	67°	75°	82°	77°
Houston, Texas	52°	69°	83°	70°
Los Angeles, CA	54°	58°	68°	65°
San Francisco, CA	48°	55°	62°	61°
St. Paul, Minnesota	12°	45°	71°	50°
St. Louis, Missouri	31°	56°	78°	59°
Cleveland, Ohio	26°	48°	71°	41°
Juneau, Alaska	23°	38°	55°	41°
Honolulu, Hawaii	72°	74°	80°	78°
New York City, NY	32°	52°	76°	47°
Washington, DC	35°	56°	78°	59°
Chicago, Illinois	22°	48°	71°	53°

How Hot?

(° is the symbol for degrees)

Fahrenheit Scale

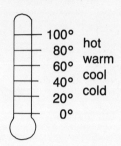

100° hot
80° warm
60° cool
40° cold
20°
0°

A. Look at the chart and the diagram. For each statement below, write _T_ if it is true, write _F_ if it is false, and write _?_ if the chart and diagram do not give you enough information. The first two are done for you.

___T___ 1. The coldest January temperature is in St. Paul, Minnesota.

___?___ 2. It is windy in Chicago in January.

_____ 3. The temperature in Honolulu doesn't change much during the year.

_____ 4. It is hot in Juneau, Alaska, in July.

_____ 5. The yearly temperature in New York City varies from 32° to 76°.

_____ 6. There is a lot of snow in St. Louis, Missouri, in January.

_____ 7. Summers in Miami, Houston, and Honolulu have temperatures in the 80s.

_____ 8. A cool place to be in the summer is Cleveland, Ohio.

_____ 9. Temperatures often reach 100° in the summer in Washington, DC.

_____ 10. Temperatures in October in Los Angeles and New York are about the same.

B. The chart shows average temperatures. To compute the average of something, you add the numbers and divide by the number of items.

Example: Add 67 + 48 + 32. The total is 147.
         Divide the total, 147, by 3. The average is 49.

Now compute these average temperatures.

1. Jan. 4th, 31°; Jan. 11th, 17°; Jan. 18th, 25°; Jan. 25th, 8°.   AVERAGE: _____

2. July 2nd, 78°; July 9th, 98°; July 16th, 83°; July 23rd, 91°.   AVERAGE: _____

3. Oct. 5th, 71°; Oct. 13th, 66°; Oct. 20, 80°; Oct. 30th, 76°.   AVERAGE: _____

Skill Objective: Reading and computing Fahrenheit temperatures. Discuss the chart of temperatures; refer students to the Fahrenheit scale and discuss the words *warm* and *cool*; compare them with *hot* and *cold*. Ask questions such as "What is the average temperature in Miami in January? Is that warm or cold?" or "You're going to visit New York in January. What kind of clothes should you take?" *Part A:* Have students complete the items individually. *Part B:* Be sure students know how to compute averages; provide several more examples before assigning Part B.

112

Benjamin Franklin

Benjamin Franklin is a famous and important person in American history. He lived from 1706 to 1790, and he had a busy life. He was an inventor, a scientist, a writer, a newspaper publisher, and a politician.

Benjamin Franklin lived most of his life in Philadelphia. He helped that city to start its first fire department and its library, and he started a school which became the University of Pennsylvania. Franklin invented a special kind of heating stove called the Franklin stove, and he experimented with electricity in Philadelphia, also.

Benjamin Franklin helped write the Declaration of Independence. He wanted the American colonies to be free from King George and the English. Franklin signed the Declaration of Independence in 1776 in Philadelphia. In 1787, he helped write the Constitution of the United States. The United States is still governed under that Constitution.

Benjamin Franklin's hard work and patriotism made him one of America's heroes. Even today, 200 years later, millions of people remember this busy and intelligent man.

Answer the following questions. Circle the best answer.

1. Which of the following is true about Benjamin Franklin?
   a. He was only interested in politics.
   b. He always lived in Philadelphia.
   c. He had many different interests.
   d. He was a friend of King George of England.

2. How did Benjamin Franklin help the city of Philadelphia?
   a. He invented a stove.
   b. He wrote the Declaration of Independence.
   c. He brought electricity to the city.
   d. He started a library, fire department, and university.

3. In the Declaration of Independence, Americans said that they wanted to be free from
   a. Benjamin Franklin.
   b. the British.
   c. America.
   d. patriotism.

4. Benjamin Franklin is one of America's heroes because
   a. he was always very busy.
   b. he experimented with electricity.
   c. he loved his country and helped it in many ways.
   d. he published a great newspaper and lived in Philadelphia.

5. Benjamin Franklin died when he was
   a. young.
   b. 84 years old.
   c. in England.
   d. signing the Declaration of Independence.

Skill Objectives: Reading a biography; reading for detail; making inferences; learning test-taking skills. Ask students to name some important men or women in American history. Find out if they know anything about Benjamin Franklin. Before reading the passage silently, have students scan it for new vocabulary; help them to work out the meanings from context if possible. After they have read the passage, go through item 1 with them as a class, then assign the remaining items for independent work.

113

The United States Government

A. Before you read the story, look at the Vocabulary Preview. Be sure that you know the meaning of each word. Use the dictionary. Some words have more than one meaning. The way the word is used in the story will help you decide the meaning you want. Write down the meanings of the words you are not sure of.

Vocabulary Preview

government	Representatives
fair	voters
efficient	elect
power	President
branches (of government)	Vice President
responsibilities	courts
laws	protect
follow	rights

B. Now read the story. Use the dictionary if there are other words that you are not sure about. Notice that the words from the Vocabulary Preview are underlined.

The Branches of the United States Government

The Constitution of the United States is the plan for the American government. Important American leaders, including George Washington, James Madison, Alexander Hamilton, and Benjamin Franklin, wrote the Constitution in 1787. The writers wanted to build a fair and efficient government for the new nation. They wanted to be sure that no one person or group of people held all the power. Therefore, they planned a government with three branches, or separate parts. They divided the powers and responsibilities of government between these three branches.

The first branch of the United States government is the *legislative branch.* This is the branch that makes the laws. The second branch is the *executive branch.* This is the branch that carries out the laws. The third branch is the *judicial branch.* This is the branch that tells what the laws mean. It also makes sure that people follow the laws.

In the United States government, the legislative branch is the Congress. There are two parts of Congress, the Senate and the House of Representatives. The men and women in the Senate are called Senators. American voters choose them. Senators serve for six years. There are two Senators for each state in the United States. This means that there are 100 Senators.

The men and women in the House of Representatives are called Representatives. American voters elect them also. They serve as Representatives for two years. There are 435 Representatives in the Congress. States with many people have many Representatives. States with few people have few Representatives.

The President and Vice President are in the executive branch. They have many thousands of people to help them carry out the laws and run the government. Americans elect the President and Vice President every four years.

The judicial branch is the Supreme Court and other courts. The courts decide what a law means and if it follows the Constitution or not. All laws have to follow the Constitution. The courts make sure that people follow the laws. In this way, they protect the rights of all Americans.

(Go on to the next page.)

Skill Objectives: Reading comprehension; building vocabulary. Allow time for students to look up vocabulary words in the dictionary and choose the appropriate definition. Review the definitions together. If you wish, read the selection aloud before asking students to read it silently. Extension Activity: After completing the reading, ask students, "Who is the President of the U.S.? Who is the Vice President? Are they Democrats or Republicans? When is the next election? Who are the state's Senators? Who is the local Representative?"

114

C. What is the main idea of this story? Circle the best answer.

1. The Constitution tells about the American government.

2. The American government has three branches, each with different responsibilities.

3. American voters elect the President, Vice President, Senators, and Representatives.

4. The courts protect the rights of all Americans.

D. If the sentence is true, circle T. If the sentence is false, circle F.

1. James Madison was one of the writers of the Constitution.	T	F
2. The President heads all three branches of government.	T	F
3. The Senate and the House of Representatives make up the Congress.	T	F
4. The states of Texas and Vermont each have two Senators.	T	F
5. Every year, American voters choose new Representatives.	T	F
6. The President and Vice President serve for four years.	T	F
7. The Supreme Court makes new laws.	T	F

E. Some words have several meanings. What does the underlined word mean in each of these sentences? Write the number of the definition that fits, in front of each sentence.

fair— 1. not favoring one above another, honest
2. less than good, but better than poor
3. light in coloring
4. an outdoor exhibit of machinery, farm animals, etc., often with entertainment

_____ Her grades in school were only <u>fair</u>, but she was the star of the basketball team.

_____ The classroom was filled with <u>fair</u> haired children.

_____ Do you think that the tax laws are <u>fair</u>?

_____ When my family goes to the <u>fair</u>, we eat hot dogs and ride the bumper cars.

follow— 1. to go or come after
2. to walk or drive along
3. to obey, to act in accordance with
4. to watch or observe closely

_____ Did that dog <u>follow</u> you home?

_____ The court decided that the law did not <u>follow</u> the guidelines of the Constitution.

_____ Do you <u>follow</u> the World Series?

_____ <u>Follow</u> Green Street two blocks, then turn left.

Skill Objectives: Identifying main idea and details; choosing the appropriate definition. Students should complete the exercises on this page independently. Correct and discuss the answers as a class.

115

Helping You Study: Using an Index

The index of a book is a list of all the main subjects, people, and ideas talked about in the book. The index tells you what page or pages to look at to find information about a subject. It is in alphabetical order. The index is usually on the last page or pages of the book.

Here is a sample index from a short book on early American history. Look at it. Then use it to answer the questions at the bottom of the page. The first one is done for you.

Adams, John, 219, 235
Articles of Confederation, 241–242
Aztecs, 40–43

Baltimore, Lord, 139–140
Boston Massacre, 206–207
Boston Tea Party, 210–211

Cabral, Pedro, 47
Cabot, John, 47
Canada, 46, 48
Cartier, Jacques, 46, 181
Columbus, Christopher, 24, 40

Dare, Virginia, 94
Declaration of Independence, 215
De Leon, Ponce, 101
De Soto, Hernando, 83, 155

Franklin, Benjamin, 235, 249
French and Indian War, 192–193

George III, 202–203, 205

Hamilton, Alexander, 235, 244–246
Henry, Patrick, 235

Indians, 37–38, 101–102, 191–194

Jamestown, 106–135
Jefferson, Thomas, 275

Lafayette, Marquis de, 228, 230
Louisiana, 185, 186

Mason-Dixon Line, 159–160
Mexico, 14, 40–45, 47, 178–179
Montezuma, 41, 43

New England, 164–166

Penn, William, 153–155
Pilgrims, 145–148
Pizzaro, Francisco, 41–42
Pocahontas, 122–123

Quakers, 155–159

Revere, Paul, 215–216
Revolutionary War, 214–234

Smith, John, 117–127
Stamp Act, 199–200

Vespucci, Amerigo, 39

Washington, George, 140, 219–220, 236–237, 244

On what page(s) is there information about:

1. Jacques Cartier   *46, 181*

2. Benjamin Franklin   _____

3. The Revolutionary War   _____

4. Alexander Hamilton   _____

5. Mexico   _____

6. Jamestown, Virginia   _____

7. Francisco Pizzaro   _____

8. The Mason-Dixon Line   _____

9. The Articles of Confederation _____

10. The Pilgrims   _____

11. Amerigo Vespucci   _____

12. Ponce De Leon   _____

13. Marquis de Lafayette   _____

14. Virginia Dare   _____

Skill Objective: Using a book index. Read the explanatory paragraph aloud. Locate and discuss the answer to the first two questions as a class, then assign the page for independent work. Extension Activity: Have students work in pairs with the index of a science or social studies text book. Students should ask each other questions, "On what page(s) is there information about . . .?" Both partners should then turn to those pages and see if they can locate the promised information.

Places and People

A. Use words from the Data Bank to complete each of the sentences. The first one is done for you.

1. People play football in a _stadium_ .

2. People take out books from a _____ .

3. Men and women play tennis on a _____ .

4. You can find a doctor in a _____ .

5. Children play baseball on a _____ .

6. People swim in a _____ .

7. You can buy nails in a _____ .

8. You play golf on a _____ .

D A T A B A N K

clinic	diamond	golf course	hardware store
library	pool	stadium	tennis court

B. Now do these sentences the same way. Use words from the Data Bank. The first one is done for you.

1. A _mail carrier_ is a person who delivers letters.

2. A _____ is a person who repairs sinks.

3. An _____ is a person who designs buildings.

4. A _____ is a person who sells meat.

5. A _____ is a person who tells funny jokes.

6. A _____ is a person who takes care of children.

7. An _____ is a person who writes books.

8. An _____ is a person who puts lights in your home.

D A T A B A N K

architect	author	babysitter	butcher
comedian	electrician	mail carrier	plumber

Skill Objectives: Using *who* clauses; building vocabulary. Have students complete this page independently. Suggest that they use the test-taking technique described on page 94, completing the easy items first, checking off the answers, then returning to the difficult items and choosing among remaining answers. Extension Activity: Students can write completion exercises for their classmates: "A _____ is a person who . . ." "A _____ is a place where . . ." Additional location and occupation vocabulary can be found on pages 19, 30, 37, 96, 101 and 102.

117

Find the Ending

Match the beginning of each sentence with its ending. Write the letter of the ending in the blank. Be careful! Some sentences may have more than one possible "correct" ending, but you can use each letter only once. The first one is done for you.

1. A stadium is a place where ___e___

2. Libraries are places where _____

3. An astronaut is a person who _____

4. A zebra is an animal that _____

5. An encyclopedia is a set of books that _____

6. An ostrich is a large bird that _____

7. Mayors are people who _____

8. A governor is a person who _____

9. A skunk is an animal that _____

10. February is the month that _____

11. A restaurant is a place where _____

12. Movie stars are people who _____

13. Toyotas are cars that _____

14. Brazil is a country where _____

15. A saw is a tool that _____

16. Whales are large animals that _____

17. The 4th of July is a holiday that _____

18. Baseball is a sport that _____

19. Christopher Columbus is the man who _____

20. Tortillas are a food that _____

a. Portuguese is the official language.

b. has 28 days.

c. people play in the summer and fall.

d. runs a state.

e. people play sports.

f. people use to cut wood.

g. travels in a rocket ship.

h. come from Japan.

i. contains lots of information.

j. live in the ocean.

k. cannot fly.

l. celebrates America's independence.

m. run cities.

n. comes from Mexico.

o. has black and white stripes.

p. sailed to the New World in 1492.

q. waiters and waitresses work.

r. make a lot of money.

s. smells awful when it is angry.

t. you can find books on all subjects.

Skill Objectives: Reading comprehension; understanding adjective clauses with *who, where, what.* This exercise deliberately includes several possible completions for many of the sentence starters. The trick is to use each ending once. Remind the students to work in pencil as they may need to revise their answers several times. You may wish to let students work in pairs on this page.

Dear Dot

Dear Dot—

I am a girl who has a problem. I like a boy who works in a supermarket. He has to work until 10:00 every Friday and Saturday night. I have parents who are very strict and I have to be home at 10:00 on Friday and Saturday nights. I can't go out at all on school nights. I think you can understand my problem. I really like this boy but we only see each other at school. What can I do?

Melissa

1. Where does Melissa's boyfriend work? _____

2. Until what time does he work every Friday and Saturday night? _____

3. What rules do Melissa's parents have about her going out? _____

_____

_____

4. When can Melissa and her boyfriend see each other? _____

_____

5. What does the word *strict* mean in this letter? Circle the best answer.

   a. tough   b. friendly   c. quiet   d. thin

6. What is your advice to Melissa? Write Dot's answer to her.

   Dear Melissa _____ ,

   _____

   _____

   _____

   _____

   _____

   _____

   _____

                                                    _____

Skill Objectives: Reading comprehension; understanding words through context; making judgments; writing a letter. Have students read Melissa's letter independently and answer questions 1–5. Correct these items as a class. Then have students discuss what advice to give Melissa. Have any of them been in similar situations? How did they solve them? Finally, have each student write his or her advice to Melissa.

119

Vocabulary Review

Complete each sentence with a word from the Data Bank.

1. My _____ country is Vietnam.

2. Susan B. Anthony _____ a strong woman.

3. The mailcarrier _____ the mail two hours ago.

4. Paul's dog is sick; he's taking it to the _____ .

5. The policeman stopped the _____ so we could cross the street.

6. Thanksgiving is one of my favorite _____ .

7. _____ house is around the corner on the left.

8. Due to a storm the plane _____ two hours late.

9. I'm not sick at all; the doctor said I'm very _____ .

10. Peter _____ his bike six miles every day.

11. The boss _____ at me because I was late.

12. Mr. Salerno is _____ to lose some weight.

13. Several of my friends are _____ Chicago.

14. Alaska, Texas, and California are large _____ .

15. It _____ snows in Hawaii.

16. You don't need a jacket; it's _____ out.

17. We were _____ bread when the telephone rang.

18. Billy dropped the glass and _____ it.

19. The boys _____ like painting or skiing.

20. Lions and tigers are _____ animals.

D A T A   B A N K

arrived	don't	Martin's	shouted	veterinarian
baking	from	native	states	warm
broke	healthy	never	traffic	was
delivered	holidays	rides	trying	wild

Skill Objective: Vocabulary Review. The following four pages present a review of important vocabulary introduced at this level. You may wish to complete the first one or two items as a group, before assigning the page as independent work.

Vocabulary Review

Complete each sentence with a word from the Data Bank.

1. Please write your _____ on the line.

2. I went to the bank to _____ my check.

3. Her secretary _____ the report yesterday.

4. The doctor saw twelve _____ in the last three hours.

5. The baskets are full of trash; please _____ them.

6. Javier _____ misses basketball practice.

7. Betty _____ a terrible toothache yesterday.

8. Did you ride in Bob's _____ ?

9. Don't be late for your _____ .

10. Mrs. Lee told a funny _____ at the party.

11. My sister is _____ her wedding for June.

12. We took a wonderful _____ in Colorado.

13. The nurse took my _____ and it was 99.5.

14. These books must _____ about twenty pounds!

15. Sammy got to class late because he had a _____ tire.

16. It started to rain when I was _____ the house.

17. Jack _____ all his shirts last night.

18. Miriam _____ when she is near a cat or dog.

19. The newspaper photographer _____ Leo's picture.

20. The pilot told the passengers to _____ their seatbelts.

DATA BANK

address	fasten	jeep	planning	took
appointment	flat	joke	seldom	typed
cash	had	painting	sneezes	vacation
empty	ironed	patients	temperature	weigh

Vocabulary Review

Complete each sentence with a word from the Data Bank.

1. Spring and fall are my favorite _____ .

2. Maria wears beautiful _____ .

3. The mechanic _____ our car last Tuesday.

4. A waitress _____ meals in a restaurant.

5. Please put your _____ on this line.

6. In an emergency it's important to stay _____ .

7. I _____ go to the library to study.

8. The carpenter _____ have the tools he needs.

9. Pedro _____ weights at the gym every day.

10. Tina invited two hundred fifty people to her _____ .

11. Gloria _____ Yale University last year.

12. Did you eat the _____ pizza?

13. John was feeling _____ after he watched a horror movie.

14. The weather in autumn is usually _____ .

15. Let's drive; it's _____ far to walk to the museum.

16. Last winter we _____ on the frozen pond for hours.

17. Larry will work _____ when he graduates.

18. I was so tired that I _____ until 11:30.

19. We were _____ for the bus when the fire started.

20. The U.S. government has three separate _____ .

D A T A B A N K

attended	clothes	full-time	serves	too
branches	doesn't	lifts	signature	waiting
calm	fixed	often	skated	wedding
cool	frightened	seasons	slept	whole

Vocabulary Review

Put the words from the Data Bank into the correct boxes.

Occupations	Feelings	"How Often" Words
1. _____	1. _____	1. _____
2. _____	2. _____	2. _____
3. _____	3. _____	3. _____
4. _____	4. _____	4. _____
5. _____	5. _____	5. _____

Irregular Verbs	Geography Words	Weather Words
1. _____	1. _____	1. _____
2. _____	2. _____	2. _____
3. _____	3. _____	3. _____
4. _____	4. _____	4. _____
5. _____	5. _____	5. _____

Law and Government	Money and Banking
1. _____	1. _____
2. _____	2. _____
3. _____	3. _____
4. _____	4. _____
5. _____	5. _____

⊡ⒶⓉⒶ ⒷⒶⓃⓀ DATA BANK

always	court	go	often	sometimes
angry	desert	interest	plain	sunny
break	deposit	jealous	proud	temperature
cashier	disappointed	lawyer	river	take
check	electrician	maid	representative	volcano
cloudy	embarrassed	model	savings account	vote
computer programmer	Fahrenheit	mountain	seldom	withdraw
Constitution	freezing	never	sleep	write

End of Book Test: Completing Familiar Structures

Circle the best answer.

Example: He _____ play soccer.

(a. can)   b. is   c. knows   d. do

1. Bob _____ to work tonight.

   a. have   b. has   c. did   d. does

2. Do you like _____ Chinese food?

   a. eat   b. to eating   c. to eat   d. eats

3. _____ Mrs. Jones take the bus to work?

   a. Do   b. Is   c. Has   d. Does

4. My sister _____ the bus yesterday.

   a. is missing   b. miss   c. missed   d. misses

5. _____ you have chicken for dinner last night?

   a. Did   b. Do   c. Was   d. What

6. Where _____ you yesterday?

   a. were   b. was   c. did   d. are

7. _____ did the bus leave?

   a. That   b. When   c. Who's   d. How long

8. Mary didn't _____ her homework.

   a. finished   b. finishes   c. finish   d. finishing

9. I _____ when you called.

   a. slept   b. was slept   c. sleep   d. was sleeping

10. Reporters are people who _____ the news.

    a. write   b. writes   c. are write   d. writing

11. My teacher usually _____ papers in the evening.

    a. correct   b. correcting   c. corrects   d. are correct

12. My father _____ want to wash the dishes.

    a. don't   b. doesn't   c. do   d. isn't

Fannee Doolee's secret (See page 15) Fannee Doolee likes words with double letters. She doesn't like words without double letters. Carlos likes words that end in s.

Skill Objective: End of Book Test. See annotation on page 124.

End of Book Test: Completing Familiar Structures (continued)

13. How many hours _____ they work last week?
    a. does   b. can   c. did   d. do

14. Lidia cleans her room but her brothers _____.
    a. doesn't   b. don't   c. didn't   d. aren't

15. Hairdressers _____ hair.
    a. cut   b. cuts   c. to cut   d. cutting

16. Do you want _____ a movie?
    a. to seeing   b. see   c. seeing   d. to see

17. We're going to _____ favorite restaurant tonight.
    a. us   b. our   c. ours   d. we

18. Larry doesn't _____ in class.
    a. listen   b. listens   c. listening   d. to listen

19. My teacher _____ to class early.
    a. seldom comes   b. comes seldom   c. seldom is coming   d. is seldom coming

20. When is your father going to visit you? _____.
    a. Last week   b. Two days ago   c. Yesterday   d. Tonight

21. Carlotta never _____ her exercises.
    a. is doing   b. to do   c. doing   d. does

22. Were you in New York last week? No, I _____.
    a. weren't   b. didn't   c. am not   d. was not

23. How many children _____?
    a. does Lucy has?   b. has Lucy?   c. does Lucy have?   d. does have Lucy?

24. How many years did Henry attend school? He _____ school for five years.
    a. did attend   b. was attending   c. attend   d. attended

25. My mother _____ lunch when I came home from school.
    a. make   b. was making   c. is making   d. makes

What's the Problem? (See page 74) Answers: 1. *42;* 2. *60%* 3. *1/3;* 4. *4 cups;* 5. *$234.46;* 6. *82;* 7. *$16.02;* 8. *110 pounds;* 9. *250 miles;* 10. *55* 11. *1,2,5,10,25,50* 12. *8*

End of Book Test: Writing Questions

Example: William goes to school every day.

Where _does William go every day_ ?

1. Mary wants to be a veterinarian when she grows up.

   What _____?

2. Mr. Smith works ten hours a day.

   How many _____?

3. Mr. and Mrs. Carlson went to the baseball game yesterday.

   Where _____?

4. Kathy washed her car yesterday.

   What _____?

5. My brothers like to play the guitar.

   What _____?

6. John and Paul are going to college in two years.

   When _____?

7. The bus comes at ten o'clock.

   When _____?

8. Linda sleeps in the living room.

   Where _____?

9. It rained yesterday.

   When _____?

10. Peter was sleeping when I called him.

    What _____?

11. Sam feels terrible.

    How _____?

12. Susan paid $2000 for her new car.

    How much _____?

Skill Objective: End of Book Test. Go over the directions and example with the class. Point out that the first word(s) of each question is/are provided. Assign the page as independent work.

End of Book Test: Reading Comprehension

The Wedding

A bride is usually late for her wedding, so no one was nervous when Maria was ten minutes late. Her parents started to worry when they realized that she was fifteen minutes late. Miguel, her husband-to-be, started to worry too. When she was thirty minutes late all of the guests were also worried. Everyone was asking the same question, "Where is Maria?"

Finally at 10:45 a limousine appeared in front of the church. Maria was not in the long, black car. Her sister, Rosa, was the only passenger. Rosa got out of the car and walked slowly into the church. She had a white envelope with her. Rosa handed the letter to Miguel.

Everyone in the church was watching Miguel. He turned away from the crowd. He opened the letter and started to read. Suddenly Rosa started to cry. Miguel finished the letter. He turned to his family and friends. He tried to explain but no words came out of his mouth. Of course there was no need for words. The look on Miguel's face and the tears in Rosa's eyes explained everything.

A. Answer the following questions.

1. Who is usually late for a wedding? _____

   _____

2. When did Maria's parents start to worry? _____

   _____

3. What is a limousine? _____

4. What did Rosa have for Miguel? _____

5. Who watched Miguel? _____

   _____

B. Number these statements in the correct order.

_____ The limousine appeared.   _____ Rosa cried and Miguel tried to speak.

_____ Rosa carried something to Miguel.   _____ Everyone started to worry.

_____ Miguel started to worry.

C. What did the letter probably say? Circle the best answer.

a. Maria died.   c. Maria would be an hour late.

b. Maria wasn't coming.   d. Miguel was a bad man.

Skill Objective: End of Book Test. Students should read this story several times, then answer the comprehension questions. Accept factually correct short answers as well as complete sentences in Part A.

Skills Index

The pages listed below are those on which the skills are introduced and/or emphasized. Many of the skills appear, incidentally, on other pages as well.